Crafting Your Dream Craft Fair

The Ultimate Guide to Success for Artisans and Makers

Jeanelle K. Douglas

Copyright © 2024 by Jeanelle K. Douglas.

DEDICATION

To the reader who holds this book. You hold the key to unlocking this journey.

Thank you for joining me.

Contents

Introduction

Crafting Your Dream Fair

Welcome to the exciting world of craft fairs, where creativity meets commerce and communities come to life through artistic expression. If you've ever wanted to organize an event that honors craftsmen's inventiveness, nurtures local talent, and makes guests happy, you've come to the perfect spot.

Craft fairs are more than simply marketplaces; they are cultural hotspots where handcrafted treasures find new homes, producers and fans meet, and the entrepreneurial spirit thrives. Whether you're a seasoned artist looking to display your products, a passionate event organizer looking to create your own fair, or simply someone fascinated by the wonder of handcrafted items, this book is your entire guide to making your craft fair dreams a profitable reality.

In the pages that follow, we'll go on a voyage of discovery and empowerment, looking at every aspect of producing and establishing a successful craft show. Each chapter will provide you with the information, resources, and inspiration you need to establish and run your own successful craft fair business, covering rigorous planning, smart marketing, smooth event execution, and long-term development plans. But this book is more than simply a how-to manual; it's a celebration of creativity, community, and the transformational power of handcrafted art. It's an homage to the craftsmen who put their hearts and souls into their work, the organizers who work diligently to make their ideals a reality, and the customers who value the beauty of handcrafted gifts.

So, whether you want to stroll through aisles of unique handcrafted goods, imagine your own artisanal creations adorning vendor booths, or foster a vibrant community of makers and enthusiasts, let this book be your guide on the exciting journey of starting and growing your own craft fair. Prepare to release your creativity, fire your business spirit, and start on an exciting journey through the world of craft fairs.

Understanding the Craft Show Industry

The industry is essential for anybody considering starting their own craft show. Craft fairs have grown from tiny neighborhood gatherings to major cultural and economic events that draw craftsmen, dealers, and customers from all around.

Exploring the complexities of the craft fair business may provide prospective organizers with useful insights into the market dynamics, trends, and possibilities that form this thriving sector. Craft fairs provide an opportunity for craftsmen and producers to present their unique works, which range from handcrafted jewelry and textiles to pottery, carpentry, and more.

These events provide an opportunity for artists to meet potential clients, tell their stories, and form important connections with other makers and aficionados. Craft fairs help local economies by promoting small enterprises, encouraging entrepreneurship, and adding to the cultural fabric of communities.

One of the distinguishing features of the craft fair sector is its variety. Craft fairs occur in a variety of shapes, sizes, and topics to cater to a diverse range of hobbies and tastes. Some craft fairs specialize in specific crafts or artisanal processes, such as ceramics or fiber arts, while others provide a more diverse selection of handcrafted items.

Craft fairs can also vary in size, from modest artisan markets conducted in local parks or community centers to large-scale events staged in convention halls or outdoor sites. The craft fair business has grown and innovated significantly in recent years, thanks to a number of fundamental factors. The advent of e-commerce platforms and social media has increased artisans' reach, allowing them to interact with buyers outside their local markets and participate in virtual craft fairs. Customers' rising appreciation for handcrafted, ecological, and ethically sourced items has increased demand for artisanal goods, propelling the craft fair sector forward.

However, despite its numerous benefits, the craft fair sector brings problems and concerns for ambitious organizers. Craft show organizers compete fiercely for merchants, customers, and media attention. Furthermore, hosting a successful craft fair needs meticulous preparation, attention to detail, and efficient marketing methods to attract both sellers and spectators.

Anyone interested in starting their own craft fair must first understand the business. By understanding the market dynamics, trends, and opportunities that influence this thriving industry, prospective organizers can position themselves for success and provide unforgettable experiences for both craftsmen and customers.

The Advantages of Organizing a Craft Show

Starting a craft show has several benefits that go beyond monetary gain. Whether you're an artist hoping to display your products, an event organizer looking for a new endeavor, or a community member trying to encourage local talent, the benefits of organizing a craft fair are numerous and varied.

A craft fair allows craftsmen and manufacturers to present their distinctive works to a larger audience. Participating in a craft fair allows craftsmen to meet with potential consumers, get feedback on their work, and build a loyal customer base. It enables them to share their passion, story, and creative process with guests, leading to a greater appreciation for handcrafted items and artisanal craftsmanship.

Hosting a craft fair may benefit the local economy and community. Craft fairs promote small companies and local craftspeople, which helps boost the economy and create jobs. They also contribute to the preservation of traditional crafts and artisanal processes, strengthening towns' cultural fabric and instilling citizens with a sense of pride and identity. Craft fairs also function as social and cultural hubs, bringing individuals from many backgrounds together to celebrate creativity, share ideas, and form significant connections.

They offer an opportunity for craftsmen, merchants, and customers to meet, exchange experiences, and form relationships, building a sense of community and belonging. Starting a craft fair is a chance for an entrepreneur to transform a love for arts and crafts into a lucrative business. Craft fairs may produce cash via vendor fees, ticket sales, sponsorships, and goods sales, giving organizers a long-term stream of income. Furthermore, successful craft fairs may help organizers gain brand recognition and reputation, opening the door to new possibilities and enterprises in the event business.

Aside from financial benefits, organizing a craft fair allows organizers to positively influence the environment by encouraging sustainable practices and supporting eco-friendly activities. Many craft fairs stress the use of natural, recyclable, and ethically obtained materials in handcrafted items, which helps to save the environment and raises awareness about sustainable living practices.

The advantages of organizing a craft show are numerous and far-reaching. Craft fairs serve an important role in enriching communities' cultural, social, and economic fabric by giving a forum for craftsmen to present their products and encouraging community interaction, as well as promoting economic growth and environmental sustainability.

Research and Planning

Research and planning are critical components for organizing a successful craft show. They lay the groundwork for the whole event and play a critical role in its success. Effective event planning relies heavily on research. Before getting into the details of planning a craft fair, it's critical to undertake extensive research to understand the market, target audience, and competitors.

This includes selecting the craft fair's target audience, examining local demand for handcrafted items, and studying competing events to determine their strengths and limitations. Market research also includes determining trends and preferences in the craft sector. This entails keeping up with current crafts, developing trends, and understanding customer preferences.

Understanding what is popular in the market allows organizers to personalize their craft according to their target audience's interests and separate themselves from competition. Another important part of research is venue selection. Finding the correct site is critical to the success of a craft fair since it affects attendance, accessibility, and the entire experience for exhibitors and guests.

Organizers must do research and analyze possible venues using criteria like location, size, amenities, and cost. They should also consider foot traffic, parking availability, and local rules when choosing a site. After conducting research, the next stage is to plan. Planning includes creating a strategic roadmap for the craft fair and defining the objectives, goals, and activities that must be completed leading up to the event.

This involves developing a timetable with significant milestones, defining a budget, and allocating resources efficiently. One of the most crucial components of planning is creating specific goals and objectives for the craft show. This includes establishing the event's aim, such as promoting local artists, raising cash for a charitable cause, or just providing guests with a pleasant and engaging experience.

Clearly establishing goals and objectives allows organizers to stay focused and ensure that all choices and activities are consistent with the overarching vision for the craft fair. Planning also includes creating a marketing and promotion strategy to attract vendors and guests to the event. This entails establishing target promotional channels, such as social media, email marketing, and local advertising, as well as developing captivating messages and images to pique interest and enthusiasm. Organizers may also explore working with local companies, community groups, and influencers to broaden their reach and promote the craft fair to a larger audience.

Research and planning are critical elements in the process of organizing a craft show. By performing extensive research and crafting a strategic plan, organizers can build the basis for a successful event that connects with their target audience, attracts great vendors, and offers a memorable experience for all participants.

Understanding Your Target Demographic

Understanding your target demographic is an important part of running a craft show. Your target audience is the individuals or groups of people who are most likely to visit your craft fair and make purchases from the merchants. Gaining a thorough knowledge of your target audience allows you to personalize your event to their specific requirements and preferences, thus enhancing the success and profitability of your craft fair endeavor.

The first step in knowing your target audience is to undertake market research. This entails obtaining data on the demographics, hobbies, and purchasing habits of potential guests. Age, gender, income, education level, and geography are all important demographic aspects to consider. Understanding your target audience's demographics allows you to adapt your marketing efforts and craft fair products to their individual tastes and interests.

In addition to demographic information, you should research your target audience's psychographics. Psychographics are the attitudes, values, lifestyles, and personalities of people or groups. Understanding your target audience's psychographics allows you to acquire insight into their motivations, preferences, and purchase patterns. For example, some visitors may value sustainability and eco-friendliness in their shopping selections, while others may be more interested in unique and handcrafted items.

Identifying your target audience's demands and pain areas is another critical step in knowing them. What obstacles or problems does your target audience encounter, and how can your craft fair meet those needs? By recognizing and meeting the requirements of your target audience, you can promote your craft fair as a worthwhile and relevant experience for guests.

Recognizing your target audience requires knowing where and how to approach them. This involves determining the channels and platforms your target audience utilizes to learn about events and make buying decisions. For example, younger audiences may spend more time on social media platforms like Instagram and TikTok, but older audiences may prefer conventional advertising channels like newspapers and radio. Once you've identified your target demographic, you can adapt your marketing efforts to successfully reach and engage them.

This might include building targeted advertising campaigns, producing appealing language and graphics that engage with your target audience, and utilizing influencer alliances or collaborations to broaden your reach.

In short, recognizing your target demographic is critical to the success of your craft show. By conducting thorough market research, delving into your target audience's demographics and psychographics, identifying their needs and pain points, and knowing where and how to reach them, you can create a craft fair experience that resonates with attendees while also driving success for vendors and organizers.

Assessing Market Demand

Assessing market demand is an important phase in the process of organizing a craft show. It entails carefully assessing the degree of interest and demand for handcrafted items in the target market, as well as identifying any potential gaps or openings that the craft fair may fill. Having a thorough grasp of market demand allows organizers to make educated judgments regarding the viability and possible success of their craft fair enterprise.

Conducting market research is one of the most common ways to estimate market demand. This entails obtaining information and insights about potential attendees and consumers' tastes, behaviors, and purchase habits. Surveys, focus groups, interviews, and observations are all methods of gathering information directly from the target audience. Furthermore, organizers may use current market data, industry studies, and trends to obtain insight into larger market trends and customer preferences for handcrafted items.

In addition to obtaining qualitative and quantitative data, organizers can analyze market demand by assessing the amount of competition in the surrounding region. This includes investigating current craft fairs, artisan markets, and comparable events to learn about their offers, target customers, and success rates. Identifying the strengths and shortcomings of rival events allows organizers to understand how to position and differentiate their craft fair in order to attract guests and merchants.

Understanding the craft industry's seasonal and cyclical character is also important when determining market demand. Craft fairs and artisan markets frequently see swings in demand due to holidays, seasons, and regional events. To optimize attendance and engagement from both vendors and spectators, organizers must consider these variables when deciding when and how frequently to hold their craft fair.

Organizers can gauge market demand by soliciting interest and comments from potential vendors and artists. By engaging with local craftsmen and merchants through outreach activities, networking events, and online groups, organizers may better understand their needs, preferences, and expectations for participation at a craft fair. By requesting feedback and suggestions from potential exhibitors, organizers may personalize the craft fair experience to their specific needs and ensure a successful collaboration.

Measuring market demand necessitates a multidimensional strategy that incorporates quantitative data, qualitative insights, competitive research, and input from potential suppliers and attendees.

Analyzing Competition

Analyzing competition is an important part of creating a craft fair since it gives useful insights into the current environment of comparable events and helps organizers understand how to position their craft fair for success. Studying competition involves investigating and finding current craft fairs, artisan markets, and comparable events in the immediate vicinity or region. This involves investigating their services, such as the sorts of exhibitors and items available, the event structure and programming, and the target population they serve.

Understanding the strengths and shortcomings of rival events allows organizers to acquire useful insights into what works effectively in the industry and discover areas where their craft fair can stand out to attract guests and merchants.

Examining competition means determining the success and popularity of competing activities. This includes evaluating attendance figures, vendor involvement, consumer happiness, and media attention. Organizers can determine the potential market size and possibility for their own event by analyzing the amount of demand and interest in existing craft fairs. Competitive analysis entails finding competitor events' unique selling features (USPs) and value propositions.

This involves learning what distinguishes them from competitors in the industry and why attendees and vendors prefer to attend their events. Identifying the USPs of rival events allows organizers to understand how to position their craft fair so that it offers something unique and appealing to their target audience.

However, studying competitiveness necessitates comparing the pricing and fee structures of rival events. This includes calculating vendor fees, admission tickets (if applicable), and any other expenses related to participating or attending. Understanding other events' pricing tactics allows organizers to determine how to price their own event competitively while maintaining profitability and value for suppliers and guests.

In addition, organizers can assess competitiveness by soliciting comments and ideas from potential suppliers and guests. Organizers can learn about local artists, producers, and community members' preferences, expectations, and pain points associated with participating in or visiting craft fairs by conducting surveys, focus groups, or one-on-one talks. By obtaining input from the target audience, organizers may successfully adjust the craft fair experience to their requirements and preferences.

Creating a Unique Selling Proposition (USP)

Creating a unique selling proposition (USP) is critical for setting your craft fair apart from rivals and attracting exhibitors and guests. A USP is a statement that expresses the unique benefits or value proposition of your craft fair, distinguishing it from other comparable events on the market.

To create a compelling USP for your craft fair, first discover the distinguishing traits or attributes that make your event special. This might include features like vendor diversity and quality, a focus on specialized crafts or artisanal processes, participatory seminars or demonstrations, and an emphasis on sustainability and eco-friendliness.

Next, think about the requirements, preferences, and pain points of your target audience. What do they seek in a craft fair, and how does your event meet their wants or solve their concerns? By matching your unique selling point with your target audience's needs and expectations, you can craft a more engaging and relevant message that will appeal to potential vendors and attendees.

Another factor to consider while developing your USP is the whole experience and environment of your craft show. What distinguishing characteristics or qualities will make your event memorable and pleasurable for attendees? This might feature live music performances, food and beverage options, interactive activities for youngsters, or a lively and friendly community vibe. By emphasizing these experience components in your USP, you may elicit excitement and expectation from potential participants.

Consider the larger context and ideals that your craft show represents. Does your event benefit local craftsmen and small businesses? Does it encourage sustainability and environmental responsibility? Is it dedicated to strengthening community ties and appreciating cultural diversity? By incorporating these principles into your USP, you may attract guests with similar values and beliefs, fostering a sense of alignment and connection with your event.

While developing your USP, consider the language and content that will most successfully connect with your target audience. Use precise and succinct language to effectively express your craft fair's unique features and value proposition. Whether it's through taglines, slogans, or descriptive language, make sure your USP successfully conveys what makes your event unique and why attendees and vendors should attend.

Developing a unique selling proposition (USP) is critical for distinguishing your craft fair from rivals and attracting exhibitors and consumers. You can create a unique selling point for your craft fair by identifying its distinct features and attributes, aligning them with the needs and preferences of your target audience, emphasizing experiential elements and values, and using clear and compelling language.

Setting Goals and Objectives

Setting specific goals and objectives is an important step in the process of launching a craft fair because it gives a road map for organizers to clarify their vision, set quantifiable targets, and drive decision-making throughout the planning and execution phases.

Organizers must identify the craft fair's broad aims. These goals are the event's guiding principles and ultimate objectives. Goals may include promoting local artists and small companies, increasing community participation and relationships, creating cash for vendors and organizers, or displaying a varied range of handcrafted items and skills.

Organizers must break down the goals into precise, quantifiable targets. Objectives are specific and attainable goals that are consistent with the overall goals of the craft fair. They provide a clear framework for event managers to evaluate event performance and track progress toward overall goals. For example, if one of the craft fair's goals is to promote local artisans and small businesses, specific objectives might include attracting a certain number of artisan vendors to the event, generating a minimum amount of sales revenue for vendors, or facilitating networking opportunities between vendors and attendees.

Similarly, if the goal is to promote community engagement and connections, objectives could include attracting a specific number of local community attendees, hosting interactive activities or workshops that encourage participation and interaction, or gathering feedback from attendees to assess satisfaction and engagement levels.

Setting defined goals and objectives entails creating a schedule for accomplishing them. Organizers must set clear milestones and deadlines for each aim to measure progress and make modifications as needed during the craft fair's planning and implementation stages. Goals and objectives should be reasonable and attainable, taking into consideration issues like budget restrictions, resource availability, and market trends. Setting too ambitious or unrealistic goals can result in disappointment and frustration if they are not realized; thus, it is critical to strike a balance between ambition and feasibility when setting targets.

Clear communication should convey the goals and objectives to all craft fair stakeholders, including merchants, sponsors, volunteers, and visitors. Clear communication helps to coordinate everyone's efforts toward the event's common goals while also instilling a sense of accountability and teamwork among all stakeholders.

Legal Structure

The legal structure chosen for the craft show will influence several elements, including liability, taxation, fundraising, and administrative obligations. The chosen legal structure for the craft show will influence several elements, including liability, taxation, fundraising, and administrative obligations. Organizers must carefully analyze the various possibilities available and choose the structure that best suits their goals, needs, and situation.

Sole proprietorships are a frequent legal entity for hosting events such as artisan fairs. One person runs and owns the craft fair in a solo proprietorship. This structure is simple and uncomplicated because it does not require formal registration or significant paperwork. However, the organizer accepts full personal responsibility for any bills, responsibilities, or legal concerns that develop during the event. Another alternative is to organize the artisan show as a cooperation.

A partnership entails two or more people working together to execute and manage an event. Partnerships can be broad or limited, with all partners sharing equal duties and obligations. Partnerships are reasonably simple to form and provide flexibility in terms of administration and decision-making. A partnership, like a sole proprietorship, is directly accountable for the craft fair's commitments and liabilities.

Alternatively, organizers may decide to establish a limited liability corporation (LLC) for the craft show. An LLC provides organizers with personal liability protection by separating their personal assets from the craft fair's assets. This implies that, in most cases, organizers are not personally accountable for the LLC's debts, responsibilities, or legal concerns. Furthermore, organizers can select between a member-managed or manager-managed structure and determine how the LLC would be taxed, providing flexibility in terms of management structure and taxes.

Organizers of larger craft fairs or events that involve considerable financial risk may want to incorporate a company. A corporation is a distinct legal entity from its stockholders and offers the highest level of personal responsibility protection. In most cases, shareholders are not individually accountable for the corporation's debts, responsibilities, or legal concerns. Corporations, on the other hand, have greater formality and administrative procedures, such as stock issues, frequent meetings, and yearly reporting.

In addition to these basic legal forms, organizers may consider alternative choices, such as nonprofit organizations or cooperatives, based on the craft fair's unique aims and characteristics. Nonprofit organizations often serve philanthropic, educational, or community-oriented objectives and may provide tax breaks.

Cooperatives are member-owned and run organizations that prioritize the interests of their members. Organizers should carefully weigh the benefits and drawbacks of each option before seeking legal and financial guidance on the best structure for their craft show. Organizers should carefully weigh the benefits and drawbacks of each option before seeking legal and financial guidance on the best structure for their craft show.

Registering Your Craft Fair Company

Registering your craft fair company is a vital step in establishing a legal presence and complying with government rules. This procedure includes filling out the relevant paperwork and files to formally register the business with the right authorities. Registration stages and requirements for your craft fair company may vary depending on the chosen legal structure (e.g., sole proprietorship, partnership, LLC, corporation), event location, and local restrictions or licensing requirements.

Most small-scale craft fairs, particularly those organized by individuals or small groups, may be best suited to registration as a sole proprietorship or partnership. In this situation, the registration procedure usually includes getting the requisite permissions and licenses from local government agencies, such as city or county offices. The first step in registering your craft fair business is to select a business name.

It is critical to have a unique and distinctive name that appropriately describes the nature of your craft show. After deciding on a name, you must check its availability and ensure that no other business in your region is currently using it. The next step is to register your business name with the proper government agency. This might include registering a "doing business as" (DBA) or fake name with your local county clerk's office or business registration agency. This step assures that your craft fair business may legally function under the name you've selected.

In addition to registering your company name, you may be required to seek additional permissions or licenses based on the nature of your craft fair and local requirements. This may include temporary event permits, health and safety permits, food handling permits (if food vendors are present), or permissions for outside signs or buildings. If you've decided to run your craft fair as a formal business organization, such as an LLC or corporation, you'll need to submit additional paperwork and forms to register with the state. This usually entails filing articles of formation or incorporation with the relevant state agency, along with any applicable costs.

After registering your craft fair business, you must continue to fulfill any ongoing reporting and compliance obligations. This may involve submitting yearly reports, renewing permits or licenses, and meeting any tax or regulatory requirements.

Obtaining Licenses and Permissions for Your Craft Company

Obtaining the proper permissions and licenses is an important part of organizing a craft fair since it assures legal compliance and protects organizers from any fines, penalties, or shutdowns. The particular permissions and licenses necessary will vary based on the location of the event, the size and scale of the craft fair, and the sorts of activities and merchants participating.

Here's a thorough look at the process of getting the required permissions and licenses for a craft fair:

1. Research local legislation: Begin by investigating the local legislation and requirements for events and temporary gatherings in the region where you intend to hold the craft fair. Inquire with local or county government authorities, such as the permits or licensing department, about the precise permissions and licenses necessary to have a craft fair.

2. Event permission: In most circumstances, organizers must get event permission or a special events permit from local government officials. This permission permits organizers to lawfully stage the craft fair while also ensuring compliance with zoning, health, and safety standards. The application procedure for an event permit may entail providing extensive information regarding the event, such as the date, venue, projected attendance, setup, and activities.

3. Health and Safety Licenses: Depending on the activities and merchants involved in the craft fair, organizers may be required to get health and safety licenses. This is especially necessary if food sellers are present, since they may need additional permissions for food handling and preparation. Health and safety licenses guarantee that vendors adhere to cleanliness and hygiene regulations, therefore protecting guests' health and safety.

4. Vendor Licenses: To sell their items at a craft fair, merchants may be required to get particular licenses or permissions. This might include basic company licenses, sales tax permits, or permissions for specific sorts of commerce (such as handcrafted goods, food, and alcohol). Before merchants participate in the craft fair, organizers should speak with them about any licensing needs and check that they are in compliance.

5. Temporary Use Permits: If the craft fair will take place in a public park, recreation area, or other public space, organizers may need to get a temporary use permission or special event permit from the local parks and recreation department or other appropriate authorities. This permit allows you to utilize the venue for the event and may contain restrictions for setup, cleaning, and liability insurance.

6. Signs and Advertising Licenses: If organizers want to show signs or advertise the craft fair in public places using banners, posters, or other items, they may be required to get signage and advertising licenses. These permits ensure that signs and advertising materials comply with municipal requirements in terms of placement, size, and usage.

7. Alcohol Permissions: If alcohol will be served or sold at the craft fair, the organizers must secure the appropriate permissions and licenses for sales and consumption. This usually entails acquiring a temporary liquor license or special event permit from the local alcohol control board or regulatory body.

8. Fire and Safety Inspections: Depending on the size and nature of the craft fair, organizers may need to arrange for fire and safety inspections to guarantee compliance with fire codes and safety standards. This may entail evaluating tents, buildings, electrical wiring, and other equipment to verify they fulfill safety requirements.

9. Insurance Coverage: In addition to permits and licenses, organizers should look into liability insurance for the craft fair. Liability insurance protects event organizers from any accidents, injuries, or property damage that may occur during the event, therefore mitigating financial risks.

Collecting the proper permissions and licenses is an important step in planning a craft fair and ensuring legal compliance with local legislation. By studying and understanding the individual permission and licensing requirements in their region, organizers may design and execute a successful and legally compliant event that is both safe and entertaining for guests and vendors.

Understanding Tax Requirements

Understanding tax requirements is critical when organizing a craft fair, as organizers must comply with numerous tax rules and regulations at the municipal, state, and federal levels. Failure to satisfy tax responsibilities may result in penalties, fines, or legal ramifications.

Here's an in-depth look at the tax implications for craft show organizers:

1. Sales Tax: Craft fair organizers are normally in charge of collecting and remitting sales tax on behalf of merchants selling taxable products at the event. This often comprises handcrafted goods, artwork, crafts, and other physical objects offered by merchants. The sales tax rate and requirements differ by place; therefore, organizers should investigate the relevant sales tax rules and regulations in their area.

2. Vendor Sales Tax Permits: Some jurisdictions require sellers at craft fairs to get sales tax permits or licenses from the state revenue department or tax agency. Organizers should contact suppliers about their sales tax duties and make sure they understand any procedures for getting and maintaining sales tax permits.

3. Income Tax: Craft fair organizers may be required to pay income tax on event proceeds. Craft fair organizers must report cash generated from vendor booth fees, ticket sales, sponsorships, and other sources of income. Organizers should keep precise records of the craft fair's income and costs in order to appropriately report it on tax returns.

4. Employment Taxes: If the organizers hire workers or independent contractors to help with the craft fair, they may be required to withhold and return payroll taxes such as federal income tax, Social Security tax, and Medicare tax. Additionally, organizers must comply with employment tax reporting and filing regulations, such as sending W-2 forms to employees and completing Form 941 with the IRS.

5. State and Local Taxes: In addition to sales and income taxes, craft fair organizers should be aware of any additional state and local taxes that may apply. This may include venue rental income taxes, business licensing taxes, transient occupancy taxes (for events conducted in hotels or convention centers), and other local charges or levies.

6. Tax Deductions and Credits: Organizers may be entitled to tax breaks or credits on expenditures incurred while planning and running the craft fair. This might include deductions for venue rental fees, marketing and advertising charges, equipment rentals, insurance premiums, and other business-related expenses. In addition, organizers should speak with a tax consultant to discuss potential tax-saving tactics and possibilities.

7. Record-Keeping Requirements: To comply with tax duties, organizers must keep accurate and thorough records of income, costs, and any craft fair-related financial transactions. This involves preserving receipts, invoices, bank statements, and other evidence to back up income and cost deductions on tax forms. Good record-keeping systems not only assure tax compliance but also enable organizers to analyze financial performance and make educated business decisions.

Craft fair organizers must understand their tax duties in order to comply with tax rules and regulations and avoid any legal and financial penalties. Organizers may successfully manage their tax duties and conduct a legally compliant craft fair by being familiar with sales tax, income tax, employment taxes, state and local taxes, tax deductions, record-keeping requirements, and other tax issues.

Craft Fair Regulations and Procedures

Craft fair regulations and procedures are an important part of running a successful and orderly craft show. These rules and standards assist in setting clear expectations for vendors, attendees, and other participants, resulting in a safe, fair, and pleasurable event for all involved.

When developing fair rules and policies, organizers should examine all parts of the event, such as vendor requirements, booth setup instructions, a code of behavior for attendees, and methods for resolving any disputes or concerns that may emerge during the event.

Here's a full explanation of the factors involved in developing fair laws and policies:

1. Vendor Requirement: Establish clear criteria and regulations for merchants at the craft show. This may include vendor selection requirements such as acceptable product kinds, quality standards, and adherence to handcrafted or artisanal criteria. Outline standards for booth setup, such as size limits, display requirements, and safety laws.

2. Booth Assignments: Specify the procedure for distributing booth spaces to vendors, including any criteria or variables used in the allocation process. Clearly explain booth reservation deadlines, payment schedules, and cancellation procedures to vendors to guarantee a smooth and orderly booth assignment process.

3. Code of Conduct for Vendors and Attendees: Outline the code of conduct that merchants and attendees are required to follow during the craft fair. This might contain standards for professional conduct, respect, and proper relationships with other participants and attendees. Emphasize the significance of fostering a welcoming and inclusive atmosphere that values respect and diversity.

4. Establish product standards: Set guidelines for the types of products that can be sold at the craft fair, including restrictions on mass-produced items, counterfeit goods, and those that violate copyright or trademark laws. Communicate any particular product categories or themes that are consistent with the general concept or emphasis of the craft fair.

5. Booth Setup and Display Guidelines: Provide merchants with guidelines and recommendations for booth setup and display. This might include restrictions for signage, branding, pricing, and promotional materials. Encourage sellers to design visually appealing and unified displays that successfully promote their items while also improving the overall appearance of the craft fair.

6. Safety and Security Measures: Put in place safety and security measures to protect the safety of all craft fair participants and guests. This might contain rules for emergency procedures, first aid supplies, fire safety precautions, security staff, or steps to avoid theft or vandalism.

7. Dispute Resolution Protocols: Develop clear protocols for resolving disagreements or conflicts that may emerge between vendors, attendees, or other participants at the craft fair. Designate specific points of contact or assign a dedicated staff member to resolve concerns and ensure fair and prompt handling of disagreements.

8. Compliance with Laws and Regulations: Make certain that all fair rules and policies are in accordance with the applicable laws, regulations, and permits regulating events and temporary gatherings in the region. This includes following health and safety standards, sales tax requirements, zoning rules, and any other legal needs specific to the craft fair.

9. Communication and Enforcement: Communicate fair rules and regulations to all participants, including vendors, sponsors, volunteers, and attendees, using a variety of channels such as the event website, vendor agreements, informative brochures, and event venue signs. Enforce fair regulations and procedures regularly and fairly to keep the craft fair atmosphere positive and orderly.

Creating fair rules and regulations includes defining clear standards and expectations for vendors, attendees, and other participants in order to provide a safe, fair, and pleasurable experience for all parties. Organizers can create a well-organized and successful craft fair by addressing a variety of issues, such as vendor requirements, booth assignments, a code of conduct, product guidelines, safety measures, dispute resolution procedures, compliance with laws and regulations, and communication and enforcement.

Venue Selection and Logistics

Venue selection and logistics are critical components of planning a successful craft fair since they have a direct influence on the overall experience for exhibitors, visitors, and organizers. The process includes carefully assessing criteria such as location, size, accessibility, facilities, layout, and logistical requirements to guarantee that the chosen site can effectively meet the goals of the craft fair.

First and foremost, organizers must select an appropriate venue for the artisan fair. This includes investigating and analyzing suitable venues based on factors such as proximity to the target audience, accessibility via public transit and major highways, parking availability, and compatibility with the event's planned date and duration. After determining a location, organizers must analyze the size and layout of the venue to ensure it can accommodate the expected number of vendors, guests, and events. Considerations may include indoor and outdoor space availability, the quantity and size of booths or display areas, and the general flow of foot circulation around the venue.

Accessibility is another crucial factor to consider when choosing a place for a craft fair. Organizers must ensure that the location is accessible to people with disabilities and adheres to applicable accessibility standards and laws. This might include providing wheelchair ramps, accessible parking spots, and other amenities to enable equitable access for all participants. The amenities and facilities offered at the location are also important aspects to consider. Organizers should determine if the location has basic amenities such as bathrooms, power, water, and trash disposal facilities. Consider if the venue has the infrastructure to meet vendor requirements, such as Wi-Fi, loading docks, and storage rooms.

Logistical issues are important when selecting a site for a craft show. Organizers must assess the event's logistical requirements, including setup and breakdown schedules, load-in and load-out methods, and any limits or prohibitions imposed by venue management. Coordination with venue staff is critical to ensuring a seamless and efficient logistical strategy that avoids interruptions and enhances event efficiency.

Organizers should consider the venue's entire mood and ambiance, since these factors can have a substantial influence on the experience of visitors and exhibitors. Natural lighting, outdoor areas, landscaping, and architectural elements may all help to create an engaging and visually appealing setting that improves the overall appearance of the craft fair.

Site selection and logistics are important components of running a successful craft show. By carefully examining aspects such as location, size, accessibility, amenities, layout, and logistical requirements, event organizers may select a venue that efficiently meets the event's demands while also providing a good and memorable experience for all attendees. Close collaboration with venue staff as well as meticulous planning are required to ensure that the craft fair runs smoothly and successfully, meeting the expectations of guests, merchants, and organizers.

Effective Negotiation

Starting a craft fair requires negotiating contracts and agreements with vendors, sponsors, venue owners, service providers, and other event stakeholders. Effective negotiation ensures that all parties are aware of their rights, obligations, and expectations, as well as helping to reduce possible disagreements or difficulties that may occur during the craft fair's preparation and implementation.

When drafting contracts and agreements for a craft fair, organizers should consider many crucial criteria to safeguard their interests and assure the event's success.

1. Scope of Services: Clearly identify the services or deliverables that each craft fair participant is expected to provide. Outline the roles of vendors, sponsors, venue owners, and service providers, as well as any specific services or goods that will be supplied.

2. Terms and Conditions: Establish the agreement's terms and conditions, such as the contract's duration, payment terms, cancellation procedures, and any other applicable restrictions. Clearly describe each party's rights and duties, as well as any penalties for noncompliance or breach of contract.

3. Fees and Payments: Work with vendors, sponsors, and other craft fair partners to determine fees and payment conditions. This might include booth rental costs for vendors, sponsorship payments for sponsors, and other financial arrangements, including revenue-sharing agreements or commission schemes.

4. Insurance and Liability: Clarify insurance and liability measures to safeguard all participants in the craft fair. This might involve establishing insurance requirements for suppliers, sponsors, and organizers, as well as resolving potential problems, including indemnity and liability releases.

5. Intellectual Property: Discuss the rights and ownership of materials, logos, designs, and other intellectual property generated or utilized in conjunction with the craft show. Ensure that all parties understand their intellectual property rights and duties and that they agree to comply with any applicable copyright, trademark, or license agreements.

6. Dispute Resolution: Develop methods for addressing any conflicts or concerns that may occur throughout the planning and execution of the craft show. This might include identifying conflict resolution processes such as mediation, arbitration, or litigation, as well as appointing a point of contact or committee to handle issues.

7. Compliance with Rules and Regulations: Ensure that all contracts and agreements adhere to the applicable rules, regulations, and permits regulating events and temporary gatherings in the region. This includes following health and safety standards, sales tax requirements, zoning rules, and any other legal needs specific to the craft fair.

8. Confidentiality and Non-Disclosure: Discuss confidentiality and non-disclosure standards to safeguard sensitive information disclosed by parties throughout the negotiation process. This might include confidentiality agreements or non-disclosure provisions to prohibit the unlawful disclosure of sensitive information or trade secrets.

Carefully writing contracts and agreements with vendors, sponsors, venue owners, service providers, and other craft fair players, organizers can set clear expectations, protect their interests, and guarantee a successful and legally compliant event. Successful negotiation and contract management require close attention to detail, efficient communication, and a comprehensive grasp of all parties' rights and duties.

Securing Insurance Coverage

Securing insurance coverage is an important part of organizing a craft fair since it protects organizers, vendors, attendees, and other stakeholders from any risks, liabilities, and unanticipated events that may happen before, during, or after the event. Insurance coverage gives financial security and peace of mind, allowing the craft fair to run efficiently and securely while mitigating the effect of any events or accidents that may occur.

When preparing a craft fair, organizers should consider the following forms of insurance coverage:

1. General Liability Insurance: General liability insurance covers physical injury, property damage, and personal injury claims that may happen during the craft show. This sort of insurance protects organizers, suppliers, sponsors, and attendees from third-party claims and lawsuits resulting from accidents, injuries, or property damage that occur during the event.

2. Property Insurance: Property insurance protects the craft fair's property from damage or loss, including event tents, tables, chairs, signs, and other equipment. This sort of insurance protects organizers from financial losses caused by theft, vandalism, fire, natural catastrophes, or other unanticipated occurrences that may damage or destroy event property.

3. Product Liability Insurance: Product liability insurance covers claims resulting from injuries or damages caused by items sold or distributed at the craft fair. This sort of insurance covers vendors and organizers for claims resulting from faulty or hazardous items, product-related injuries, or allegations of carelessness in product design or manufacture.

4. Event Cancellation Insurance: Event cancellation insurance protects against financial damages incurred if the craft show is canceled, postponed, or stopped due to unanticipated events beyond the organizer's control. This sort of insurance may cover venue rental payments, vendor booth fees, advertising expenditures, and other non-refundable event-related charges.

5. Workers' Compensation Insurance: Workers' compensation insurance protects employees and volunteers who are injured or become ill while working at the trade fair. Workers and volunteers are adequately safeguarded while taking part in the event as this insurance covers medical bills, missed income, and other expenditures related to work-related accidents or illnesses.

6. Excess Liability Insurance: Excess liability insurance, often known as umbrella insurance, offers coverage that exceeds the limitations of main liability insurance plans. This form of insurance offers additional protection against huge or catastrophic claims that exceed the coverage limitations of existing insurance policies, assisting organizers in reducing financial risks linked with prospective litigation or legal claims. Organizers must carefully assess their insurance needs and consult with an expert insurance broker or agent to obtain coverage that suits the unique risks and requirements of the craft fair.

Organizers must properly review and understand insurance plans, including coverage limitations, deductibles, exclusions, and other terms and conditions, to ensure appropriate protection against potential liabilities and risks. By obtaining comprehensive insurance coverage for the craft fair, organizers can protect themselves, vendors, attendees, and other stakeholders from financial losses, legal liabilities, and unexpected events, allowing the event to run smoothly and safely while reducing potential risks and uncertainties.

Setting up Vendor Spaces

Setting up vendor spaces at a craft fair requires careful planning and coordination to ensure that each seller has a visually appealing and functioning booth that successfully displays their items.

Setting up vendor areas begins well before the event and consists of many essential steps:

1. Booth Allocation: After selecting vendors and collecting booth fees, organizers must provide booth spaces to each vendor. Considerations for booth allocation may include vendor preferences, product categories, booth size, and specific requests.

2. Booth Layout: Create a layout design for the craft fair that includes the locations of vendor booths, aisles, entrances, exits, and other important areas. Consider traffic flow, visibility, and accessibility while creating the booth arrangement to ensure that guests have a pleasant and efficient experience.

3. Vendor Communication: Communicate with vendors in advance to offer information about their allotted booth space, such as size, location within the venue, and any particular instructions or limits

for booth setup. Encourage suppliers to study the layout plan and ask questions or express issues as required.

4. Booth Setup Guidelines : Give merchants clear rules and ideas for putting up their booths. This may include recommendations for booth design, display tactics, signage, lighting, and other components that add to a visually appealing and engaging booth. Encourage merchants to be creative and present their items in ways that suit their brand and personality.

5. Load-in and Setup Hours: Establish certain hours for merchants to enter the venue and set up their booths before the craft fair begins. Communicate these hours to vendors ahead of time, and make sure that venue personnel are accessible to help with setup and resolve any logistical concerns that may occur.

6. Booth Equipment and Supplies: Ensure that merchants have access to the equipment and resources they need to set up their booths, such as tables, chairs, tents, and signs. Coordinate with rental firms or suppliers to get booth equipment delivered and set up as needed.

7. Electrical and Lighting: If merchants need access to power or extra lighting for their booths, make sure these services are accessible and correctly configured. Coordinate with venue personnel or electricians to install power outlets or lighting fixtures

as needed, and give suppliers advice on how to properly access and use electrical services.

8. Safety and Accessibility: When designing vendor areas, put safety and accessibility first. Make sure booth construction is solid and properly anchored to avoid tipping or collapsing, especially for outdoor booths exposed to wind or bad weather. Provide clear routes and accessible adjustments so that people with disabilities can comfortably navigate the craft fair.

9. Final Inspections: Before the craft fair begins, do final inspections of vendor areas to check that booths are properly set up, in accordance with guidelines and regulations, and meeting safety requirements. Address any issues or concerns that arise throughout the inspection process, and work with suppliers to make any required modifications.

Following these procedures and providing vendors with the appropriate help, information, and resources, organizers can guarantee that vendor spaces are efficiently set up, contributing to a successful and joyful craft fair experience for merchants, attendees, and organizers alike. Close planning, communication, and attention to detail are essential for designing an appealing and effective booth arrangement that highlights the ingenuity and workmanship of participating exhibitors.

Planning, Parking and Transportation For a Craft Fair

Planning parking and transportation for a craft fair is critical to providing a smooth and seamless experience for guests, vendors, and staff. Effective preparation and coordination are required to solve the logistical issues of controlling traffic flow, ensuring appropriate parking, and providing participants with suitable mobility alternatives.

Here's how to set up parking and transportation for a craft fair:

Consider Location: Select a place that has enough parking or is conveniently accessible by public transit. To ensure that attendees have easy access, consider the venue's accessibility to main roads, highways, and public transportation lines.

Parking Management: Create a parking management strategy to optimize available parking space and reduce congestion. Designate parking spots for guests, vendors, staff, and volunteers, and use signs to clearly define entrances, exits, and designated parking zones.

Off-Site Parking: If the venue does not have enough parking, consider organizing off-site parking and shuttle services to transfer visitors to and from the event location. Identify neighboring parking lots, garages, or other off-site parking facilities, and plan shuttle times and routes to make mobility easier.

Consider providing VIP parking alternatives to sponsors, vendors, and other VIP guests who require premium parking. Designate designated parking locations near the event venue for VIP attendees and offer clear directions to these parking spaces.

Accessibility: Make parking facilities accessible to guests with disabilities by offering designated accessible parking spots near event entrances and maintaining barrier-free access routes from parking lots to event venues.

Traffic Management: Implement traffic management techniques to ensure smooth traffic flow and reduce congestion around the event location. Work with local authorities, traffic control officials, and parking attendants to regulate traffic flow, guide vehicles to approved parking locations, and maintain pedestrian safety. Encourage the use of public transportation by informing people about nearby bus stops, train stations, and other public transit choices. Collaborate with local transit providers to organize special event services or discounted prices for people going to the craft fair via public transportation.

Bicycle Parking: Make bicycle parking available for those who choose to pedal to the artisan fair. Create specific bicycle parking spaces complete with bike racks or other safe storage choices, and make sure they are easily accessible from event doors.

Rideshare Services: Collaborate with rideshare businesses to create specific drop-off and pick-up zones for guests who use ridesharing services like Uber or Lyft. Coordinate with rideshare drivers to guarantee smooth operations and reduce congestion near approved drop-off and pick-up locations.

Communication: Provide guests with parking and transit information in advance via event websites, social media platforms, email newsletters, and other communication channels. Provide clear instructions, maps, and directions to assist participants in navigating parking and transit alternatives efficiently.

Using these tactics and working together with venue management, transportation providers, and local authorities, organizers may efficiently plan parking and transit for a craft fair, ensuring a good and hassle-free experience for guests, vendors, and staff. Effective parking and transportation planning contributes to the event's overall success by reducing traffic congestion, enabling easy access, and improving the attendance experience.

Marketing and Advertising

Marketing and advertising are critical components of launching a craft fair because they help build enthusiasm, attract attendees, and motivate merchants. A well-planned marketing approach may effectively promote the craft fair, enhance exposure, and contribute to its overall success.

Here's how to market and promote a craft fair:

1. Identify the target audience: Begin by establishing the craft fair's target demographic. Consider demographic factors such as age, gender, hobbies, and geographic location to determine who is most likely to come and engage in the event.

2. Craft Clear Language: Create clear and engaging language to describe the craft fair's unique value proposition. Highlight essential elements such as the diversity of handcrafted items, artisanal workmanship, family-friendly activities, entertainment, and any event-specific attractions or highlights.

3. Use Multiple Channels: To increase exposure and engagement, reach out to potential attendees via a range of marketing platforms. Print advertising, flyers, posters, and direct mail are examples of conventional channels, whereas digital channels include social media, email marketing, event websites, and online communities.4. Social Media Marketing: Use social media channels to promote the

craft show and connect with the intended audience. Create dedicated event pages or accounts on platforms like Facebook, Instagram, Twitter, and Pinterest to publish event updates, vendor and product previews, behind-the-scenes information, and interactive postings to build buzz and enthusiasm.

5. Email Marketing: Create an email list of potential attendees and merchants, then send out frequent email newsletters or updates leading up to the craft fair. Use email marketing to provide vital event information, unique deals, vendor spotlights, and reminders about registration deadlines or special attractions.

6. Collaborate with Influencers: Work with local influencers, bloggers, or social media celebrities that have a relevant following and can help market the craft fair to their fans. Consider giving them free tickets, special access, or other benefits in return for promoting the event on their platforms.

7. Partnerships and Sponsorships: Collaborate with local companies, organizations, and community groups to promote the craft fair. Collaborate with sponsors who may offer financial help, in-kind gifts, or promotional services in exchange for brand visibility and recognition during the event.

8. Press Releases and Media Coverage: Send press releases to local media sources such as newspapers, magazines, radio stations, and

internet publications to promote the craft fair and gain media attention. Invite journalists, bloggers, and influencers to the event and provide them with press credentials or media kits to help them cover it.

9. Community Engagement: Communicate with the local community through outreach activities such as neighborhood fliers, community bulletin boards, local events, and collaborations with local companies or groups. Participate in community events or festivals to promote the craft fair and network with possible guests.

10. Visual Content and Graphics: Create visually attractive advertising materials, such as posters, brochures, banners, and digital graphics, to highlight the craft fair's distinctive offers and atmosphere. Use high-quality photographs of handmade items, artisanal handiwork, and bright event scenes to attract attention and stimulate curiosity.

11. Word-of-Mouth Marketing: Encourage word-of-mouth marketing by offering incentives to guests and merchants who share their experiences and refer friends and family to the craft fair. Provide referral discounts, freebies, or special rewards to attendees who bring new visitors, as well as merchants that suggest other artists to join.

12. Feedback and Testimonials: Gather feedback and testimonials from prior attendees, vendors, and participants to demonstrate the success and pleasant experiences of previous craft fairs. Share testimonials on social media, event websites, and advertising materials to increase credibility and trust with potential attendees and vendors.

Overall, a good craft fair marketing and promotion plan includes defining the target demographic, creating a clear message, using different marketing platforms, connecting with the community, and using partnerships and sponsorships to increase exposure and attendance. Using a complete marketing strategy, organizers may effectively promote the craft fair, attract people, and produce a successful and memorable event for all participants.

Building Strong Brand Identity

Developing a strong brand identity is critical for a craft fair since it helps to distinguish the event from others, increase recognition, and attract visitors and merchants. A well-defined brand identity includes a variety of aspects that work together to portray the craft fair's distinct personality, values, and essence.

How to Create a Brand Identity for a Craft Fair:

1. State Your Vision and Values: Start by outlining the craft fair's vision and ideals. Consider what distinguishes your event and the fundamental concepts that underpin its aim. This might involve promoting handcrafted goods, assisting local craftsmen, encouraging creativity and innovation, and recognizing community spirit.

2. Develop a Brand Story: Create a captivating brand story that conveys the craft fair's history, inspiration, and purpose. Share anecdotes, testimonials, and behind-the-scenes experiences that will connect with your target audience and elicit an emotional response to the event.

3. Select a name and logo: Choose a distinctive and descriptive name for the craft fair that accurately expresses its character and purpose. Create a unique logo that visually expresses the brand and captures its spirit. Consider colors, typefaces, graphics, and symbols that are consistent with the event's subject and style.

4. Design Visual Assets: Create visual assets such as banners, posters, pamphlets, signs, and digital graphics with the craft fair's name, logo, and brand components. Ensure design uniformity across all materials to strengthen brand identification and coherence.

5. Establish Brand Guidelines: Create brand guidelines outlining the rules and criteria for utilizing the craft fair's brand elements. Establish criteria for logo usage, color palette, typography, photography, and other visual aspects to ensure consistency and integrity throughout all marketing materials and communications.

6. Craft Messaging and Tone: Establish messaging and tone of voice that represent the brand's personality and appeal to the target demographic. Consider the language, tone, and communication style that most accurately reflect the craft fair's principles, ethos, and identity.

7. Create Brand Collateral: Create branded materials such as goods, promotional items, and gifts that include the craft fair's logo and

visual identity. This might include tote bags, t-shirts, stickers, buttons, and other mementos that guests can retain as keepsakes.

8. Utilize Social Media and Online Presence: Create a robust online presence for the craft fair using social media platforms, event websites, and digital marketing methods. Use consistent branding across all online channels to promote brand identification and provide a seamless brand experience for followers and attendees.

9. Engage with the Community: Connect with the local community and target audience through outreach, partnerships, and collaborations that are consistent with the craft fair's brand values and identity. Participate in community events, partnerships with local companies, and projects that benefit the arts and crafts community.

10. Deliver a Consistent Brand Experience: Ensure that all interactions with guests, vendors, sponsors, and stakeholders reflect the craft fair's brand identity and values. From pre-event marketing to on-site encounters and post-event follow-up, create a consistent brand experience that promotes the craft fair's identity and leaves a lasting impression.

By carefully designing a brand identity that includes the vision, values, visual components, message, and tone of voice, organizers can establish a compelling and distinctive identity for the craft fair.

A strong brand identity promotes identification, attracts attendees and merchants, and establishes a distinct market presence.

Crafting Our a Marketing Plan for a Craft Fair

Creating a thorough marketing plan for a craft fair requires strategic preparation, efficient communication, and focused promotion to attract guests and merchants, enhance awareness, and assure the event's success.

Here's how to create a marketing strategy for a craft show:

Define the aims and goals of the craft fair marketing plan: Consider your goals for the event, such as increasing attendance, attracting a varied range of vendors, generating income, fostering community participation, or supporting local workmanship.

Understand the Target Audience: Determine the craft fair's target audience, including demographics such as age, gender, interests, and geographic region. Consider the interests, requirements, and motivations of potential attendees and vendors while developing marketing strategies. Conduct market research to better understand current trends, preferences, and expectations in the craft fair business. Analyze rival events, industry journals, internet forums, social media debates, and other sources to obtain insight into market dynamics and discover areas for distinction.

Craft Messaging and Branding: Create a strong, consistent brand identity, messaging, and branding for the craft fair. Define the event's unique selling proposition (USP) and successfully convey it via multiple marketing channels to differentiate the craft fair and attract guests and merchants.

Choose Marketing Channels: Determine and choose the best marketing channels to reach your target audience and effectively promote the craft show. Consider a combination of conventional and digital marketing methods, including print ads, flyers, posters, direct mail, social media, email marketing, event websites, online communities, and local media.

Create high-quality material and assets that highlight the craft fair's brand identity, values, and services. Create visually engaging visuals, films, images, and textual material that will interest and fascinate the target audience while also communicating important event information.

Implement promotional techniques: Use smart promotional techniques to build buzz and enthusiasm for the craft show. Plan pre-event, during-event, and post-event promotional events, including competitions, freebies, sneak peeks, behind-the-scenes material, vendor spotlights, and special promotions to entice attendees and merchants.

Engage with the Community: Use community outreach, partnerships, and collaborations to connect with the local community and your target audience. Participate in local events, work with local companies, organizations, and influencers, and interact with online communities to increase awareness and interest in the craft fair. Establish key performance indicators (KPIs) and metrics to assess the efficacy of the craft fair marketing strategy. Track and analyze data like attendance, vendor registrations, website traffic, social media interaction, and income to assess marketing effectiveness and find areas for improvement.

Adjust and Optimize: Constantly monitor and assess the efficacy of the craft fair marketing plan, making modifications as appropriate to maximize outcomes. Gather comments from attendees, vendors, sponsors, and stakeholders to help refine marketing efforts and improve future craft fair events.

Following these procedures and building a smart and thorough marketing strategy will enable organizers to effectively promote the craft fair, attract guests and merchants, and assure the event's success. A well-executed marketing strategy may help to enhance exposure, develop interest, and provide a memorable and successful craft fair experience for all attendees.

Incorporating Social Media Channels into Your Craft Fair Marketing Plan

The efficient promotion and marketing of a craft show requires the use of social media channels. Social media is a strong and cost-effective approach to reaching a large audience, interacting with potential attendees and vendors, creating enthusiasm, and generating talk about the event.

Here's how to use social media channels to promote a craft fair:

1. Choose the Right Sites: Begin by determining which social media sites are most relevant to your target audience and correspond with your craft fair's aims. Consider using networks like Facebook, Instagram, Twitter, Pinterest, and LinkedIn according to your target audience's demographics, interests, and levels of involvement.

2. Create compelling material: Create engaging and visually appealing material that highlights the craft fair's distinct offers, atmosphere, and highlights. This may include photographs and videos of homemade items, behind-the-scenes looks at merchants getting ready for the event, sneak peaks at prominent artists, and interactive surveys or quizzes on making and DIY.

3. Build a Community: Encourage followers to connect and participate in order to foster a feeling of community and engagement. Respond swiftly to comments, messages, and queries, and encourage guests and sellers to share their excitement and experiences in the run-up to the craft fair. Create specific event sites or groups where fans may interact, discuss ideas, and ask questions about the event.

4. Use hashtags strategically: add relevant hashtags to your social media postings to boost exposure and reach a larger audience. Look up popular hashtags for crafts, handcrafted items, local events, and craft fair-related themes or trends. Create a unique event hashtag that attendees and vendors may use to tag their posts and interact with the event online.

5. Promote Vendor Spotlights: Use dedicated social media spotlights to highlight participating vendors and craftspeople. Feature their items, stories, and workmanship to introduce them to your audience and build enthusiasm for their presence at the craft show. Encourage merchants to share these highlights with their own followings to increase reach and visibility.

6. Share event information and announcements: Keep followers up to speed and involved by providing craft fair-related information and announcements on social media. This may contain information regarding prominent attractions, entertainment, special deals, workshop sessions, and any modifications or adjustments to the event schedule or logistics.

7. Create interactive material: Encourage audience involvement and interaction by producing interactive material such as craft fair-themed polls, quizzes, competitions, and prizes. Encourage followers to participate and share their thoughts, ideas, and experiences with their social networks, raising awareness and excitement about the event.

8. Use Paid Advertising: Think about using paid advertising choices provided by social media networks to increase your reach and target certain audience demographics. Create customized ad campaigns that promote the craft fair to people who have your intended demographics, interests, and behaviors, increasing visibility and boosting ticket sales or vendor registration.

9. Collaborate with Influencers and Partners: Work with local influencers, bloggers, artisans, and organizations that have a relevant audience to promote the craft fair on social media. Collaborate on sponsored content, influencer takeovers, or collaborative promotions to increase their reach and reputation while also attracting followers to the event.

10. Monitor and Analyze Performance: Using the analytics tools given by each platform, regularly monitor and analyze the performance of your social media campaigns. Track metrics like engagement rate, reach, impressions, clicks, and conversions to assess the success of your social media campaign and find areas for improvement.

Collaboration with Local Media

Building contacts with local media is an effective method for advertising a craft fair and earning exposure in the community. Building relationships with journalists, reporters, editors, and producers may help create media coverage, raise exposure, and draw attention to the event.

Here's how to connect with local media for your craft fair:

Understand Media Outlets: Learn about your local newspapers, periodicals, radio stations, television channels, and internet publications. Identify appropriate platforms for advertising your craft fair by researching their target demographic, content emphasis, editorial criteria, and contact information.

Identify essential connections: Find essential connections in local media outlets that cover events, arts and culture, community activities, and lifestyle stories. Find reporters, editors, producers, and journalists who have previously covered comparable events or issues like handcrafted crafts, artisanal items, or local festivals.

Personalize Outreach: Send individualized pitches and press releases to media contacts, emphasizing your craft fair's unique qualities, features, and attractions. Customize your communications to each media outlet's target demographic and editorial focus, stressing newsworthy elements, human interest tales, and local significance.

Offer special content: Provide local media outlets with behind-the-scenes content, sneak peeks, and interviews with participating craftsmen, or special news about the craft fair. Provide journalists with interesting tales, graphics, and information to help them write engaging and informative event coverage. Create press kits or media packages that include detailed information on the craft fair, such as event facts, vendor profiles, the event schedule, images, logos, and any other relevant materials. Distribute press kits to media contacts, either online or in print, to enable coverage and offer journalists the information they require to report about the event.

Invite Media to Previews: Invite local media representatives to attend preview events, press conferences, or media days leading up to the craft show. Give them unique access to the event location, meet participating vendors, taste products, and get firsthand information for their coverage.

Facilitate Interviews: Arrange interviews with event organizers, participating artisans, sponsors, or special guests to provide media outlets with unique narrative possibilities. Set up on-site or remote interviews, photo sessions, and video shoots to capture intriguing material and garner media attention. Provide press passes or media credentials to accredited journalists, reporters, photographers, and videographers who want to cover the craft show. Allow them free access to the event, specific seating sections, and dedicated press areas to help with their coverage and guarantee a great experience.

Follow Up and Express Gratitude: After sending pitches, press releases, or invites to media contacts, confirm receipt and ask about their interest in covering the craft fair. Thank them for their time and consideration, and provide any assistance, extra information, or interview opportunities that may be required to aid their coverage.

Maintain Relationships: Stay in touch with local media contacts after the craft fair, provide details on upcoming events, and offer chances for cooperation or coverage of relevant issues. Keep media contacts updated on planned projects, collaborations, and notable developments that may be of interest to their audiences. Building solid connections with local media outlets and providing them with important information, access, and resources can help you effectively market your craft fair, acquire media coverage, and improve community awareness.

Collaboration with local media may help to magnify your marketing efforts, attract a larger audience, and improve the success of your event.

Implementing Promotional Methods

Implementing promotional methods is critical to the success of a craft fair since it attracts guests, engages merchants, and generates enthusiasm about the event. A well-executed promotional strategy includes a variety of marketing methods aimed at increasing awareness, boosting ticket sales, and creating excitement about the craft fair.

Here's how to use promotional methods effectively:

Define Goals and Objectives: Begin by outlining specific goals and objectives for your advertising activities. Determine what you want to accomplish with the craft fair marketing, such as raising attendance, attracting a wide range of merchants, improving income, or encouraging community involvement.

Understand Your Audience: Gain a thorough grasp of your target audience's demographics, interests, preferences, and habits. Tailor your advertising techniques to meet the requirements and motivations of potential attendees and vendors, ensuring that your language and approaches are both relevant and attractive.

Craft Compelling Messaging: Create clear, compelling, and consistent messaging that conveys the craft fair's unique value proposition. Highlight the primary characteristics, attractions, and benefits of attending or participating in the event, stressing how it differs from other craft fairs or similar events.

Use a variety of marketing platforms to reach your target demographic successfully.

Print advertising, flyers, posters, direct mail, and local media sources are examples of conventional channels, whereas digital channels include social media, email marketing, event websites, and online communities.

Create engaging material: Create engaging and visually appealing material that grabs your audience's attention and motivates them to take action. This might include images, videos, graphics, testimonials, sneak peaks, behind-the-scenes looks, and interactive articles highlighting the craft fair's artistry, creativity, and atmosphere.

Create unique promotions, discounts, incentives, and early bird deals to encourage attendance and involvement at the craft show. Offer reduced tickets, exclusive access, bundled packages, or other incentives to promote early registration, boost ticket sales, and raise enthusiasm among potential attendees.

Collaborate with Partners: Work with local businesses, organizations, influencers, and community groups to boost your promotional efforts and reach a larger audience. Collaborate on collaborative promotions, cross-promotional initiatives, or sponsorship agreements that use each partner's network, resources, and audience to promote the craft fair.

Engage with attendees and vendors by actively participating and interacting on social media, event websites, and online forums. Respond immediately to requests, comments, and messages, and encourage guests and sellers to share their excitement and experiences in the run-up to the craft fair.

Use Influencer Marketing: Collaborate with local influencers, bloggers, artisans, and personalities with a targeted audience to promote the craft fair to their following. Collaborate on sponsored content, influencer takeovers, or collaborative promotions that use their reach, reputation, and influence to get attendees and merchants to the event.

Track and Measure Results: Use appropriate metrics and key performance indicators (KPIs) to assess the effectiveness of your promotional efforts. Monitor indicators like ticket sales, website traffic, social media engagement, email open rates, and conversion rates to assess the efficiency of your promotional initiatives and make data-driven choices to improve future efforts.

Implementing a thorough promotional plan that incorporates a clear message, targeted techniques, engaging content, smart alliances, and continual measurement and optimization may help you effectively market your craft fair, attract visitors and merchants, and assure the event's success.

Vendor Acquisition and Management

Vendor acquisition and management are critical components of running a successful craft show. This procedure entails discovering, recruiting, and supervising merchants who will display their handcrafted items during the event.

Here's a detailed description of vendor acquisition and management at a craft fair:

Identifying Potential Vendors: Begin by looking for vendors that make handcrafted goods that are consistent with the concept, style, and target demographic of your craft fair. Look for local artists, manufacturers, craftsmen, and small companies that specialize in creating one-of-a-kind, high-quality items.

Outreach and Invitation: Reach out to potential vendors via email, social media, craft forums, local artisan markets, and word-of-mouth recommendations. Send individualized invites emphasizing the benefits of participation in the craft fair, such as exposure to a specific audience, sales and networking possibilities, and a platform to present their work. Set up an application process for vendors interested in participating in the craft fair. Create an online application form or vendor registration gateway where vendors may enter their information, product photographs, descriptions, price, and other pertinent information. Establish explicit standards and criteria for selecting suppliers based on the quality, uniqueness, and applicability of their products.

Review and Selection: Carefully review vendor applications to verify that they satisfy the craft fair's requirements and standards. Consider the distinctiveness and quality of the items, brand alignment, professionalism, and market demand. Choose exhibitors that best reflect the craft fair's overall goal, theme, and style, while also ensuring diversity and variation among participating merchants.

Contract and Agreement: Once vendors have been chosen, create explicit contractual agreements stating the terms and conditions for participating in the craft fair. Create vendor agreements that include specifics like booth costs, payment deadlines, booth size and location, set-up and tear-down processes, liability and insurance requirements, and any rules or regulations governing product sales, display, and conduct at the event.

Contact and Support: Maintain open and regular contact with merchants throughout the planning phase for the craft fair. Provide vendors with specific information, resources, and assistance in preparing for the event, such as logistical details, marketing materials, promotional opportunities, and any additional services or facilities accessible to them.

Booth Allocation and Setup: Assign booth space to merchants according to their preferences, booth size needs, and availability. Create a floor design or booth arrangement that maximizes traffic flow, visibility, and accessibility for both merchants and guests. Coordinate with vendors to make booth setup easier, including giving access to electricity, tables, chairs, and other equipment as needed.

On-Site Management: Oversee vendor operations and logistics on-site at the craft fair to guarantee a smooth and successful event. Assign staff or volunteers to manage vendor check-in, booth setup, and event rules and regulations. Provide help and support to vendors during the event, responding to any difficulties or complaints in a timely and professional manner.

Facilitate sales and transactions between merchants and attendees at the craft fair. Ensure that suppliers have suitable payment processing technologies, such as cash registers, credit card readers, or mobile payment applications, to receive consumer payments. Give vendors advice and support on sales strategies, customer service, and best practices for optimizing sales prospects during the event.

Feedback and Follow-Up: After the craft fair, collect feedback from sellers to assess their experience, satisfaction, and recommendations for improvement. Conduct post-event surveys or interviews to gain information on event organization, venue facilities, attendee demographics, sales success, and overall event satisfaction. Utilize comments to discover strengths and areas for improvement in vendor acquisition and management methods for future craft fairs.

Attracting Vendors

Attracting great vendors is critical to the success of a craft fair since they enhance the entire experience and mood of the event. Quality sellers present one-of-a-kind, handmade goods that appeal to guests and help boost the craft fair's reputation.

Here's how to get great vendors for your craft fair:

1. Establish Clear Selection Criteria: Define specific criteria for selecting vendors who are consistent with the craft fair's subject, style, and target demographic. Consider product quality, originality, and workmanship, as well as suppliers' professionalism and reputation. Establish clear criteria for product categories, pricing, and branding to maintain consistency and diversity across participating merchants.

2. Create an appealing vendor package. Create an appealing vendor bundle that emphasizes the advantages and value of participating in the craft show. Include information on booth options, price tiers, promotional possibilities, amenities, and vendor support services. Clearly describe the benefits of participation, including exposure to a certain audience, prospective sales, networking possibilities, and brand recognition.

3. Contact Targeted Vendors: Identify and contact targeted vendors that offer high-quality, handcrafted items that are appropriate for your craft fair's subject and style. Look up local artisans, makers, crafters, and small companies using internet directories, social media, artisan markets, craft festivals, and word-of-mouth recommendations. Personalize your approach to vendors, emphasizing why their products are a good fit for your event and the unique opportunities available to them as participants.

4. Highlight prior accomplishments: Emphasize the prior accomplishments and pleasant experiences of sellers who have attended previous craft fairs. Share testimonials, success stories, and images from previous events to highlight the importance and legitimacy of attending your craft fair. To entice new merchants to join, highlight the variety of items, vendor ingenuity, and favorable comments from attendees.

5. Provide early registration incentives. Encourage sellers to register for the craft fair early by providing incentives such as reduced booth costs, priority booth selection, or more advertising possibilities. Create a sense of urgency and excitement surrounding early registration deadlines to encourage businesses to reserve their spots in advance.

6. Provide Marketing and Promotional Support: Assure merchants that the craft fair organizers will actively promote the event to reach a large number of potential buyers. Provide marketing and promotion assistance to vendors, such as inclusion in event advertising, social media promotion, email marketing campaigns, and highlighted listings on the event website. Highlight the craft fair's significant advertising efforts and reach to attract merchants seeking to optimize their visibility and sales prospects.

7. Promote Networking and Collaboration: Provide chances for merchants to network, cooperate, and interact with one another prior to, during, and after the craft fair. Organize vendor meet-and-greets, networking sessions, or online forums where merchants may share ideas and advice and connect with other attendees. Encourage vendor collaboration for joint promotions, cross-promotional efforts, or product partnerships to increase awareness and attract new consumers.

8. Provide Excellent Vendor Support: Ensure that sellers receive excellent support and help from the craft fair organizers throughout the process. Provide suppliers with specialized advice on booth setup, logistics, marketing ideas, sales approaches, and best customer service practices. Respond to any questions, complaints, or special requests from vendors in a timely and professional manner to guarantee a great experience for all participants.

9. Emphasize Community and Collaboration: Emphasize the sense of community, camaraderie, and collaboration among sellers as a distinguishing feature of attending the craft fair. Highlight the chance for sellers to join a thriving network of local artisans, manufacturers, and craftspeople that share a passion for creativity and workmanship. Showcase testimonials and anecdotes from previous exhibitors about the craft fair's friendly and collaborative atmosphere to attract new merchants looking to join a pleasant and inviting community.

By implementing these strategies and creating an appealing and supportive environment for vendors, organizers can successfully attract high-quality vendors to their craft fair, improve the overall quality and reputation of the event, and provide a positive experience for both vendors and attendees.

Creating Clear Vendor Criteria

Creating clear vendor criteria is critical to having a successful and pleasant craft fair experience for both exhibitors and organizers. These guidelines describe the expectations, rules, and restrictions that vendors must follow before, during, and after the event.

Here's how to create excellent vendor guidelines:

1. Booth Setup and Design: Establish rules for booth setup and design to provide a visually appealing and consistent layout across the craft show. Please provide booth dimensions, space allocation, display height constraints, and any other needs or limitations. Encourage merchants to design visually appealing displays that effectively highlight their items while being clean and orderly.

2. Product Quality and Authenticity: Establish criteria for the quality, authenticity, and workmanship of objects offered at the craft show. Require vendors to produce or create all items and ensure they meet specified standards for uniqueness, inventiveness, and workmanship. Prohibit the sale of mass-produced or commercially made things in order to keep the event's distinctive and artisanal essence.

3. Product Categories and Diversity: Establish distinct product categories or themes that are consistent with the general idea and style of the craft fair. Encourage vendor diversity by offering a variety of product kinds, styles, and pricing points to appeal to a wide range of guests. Avoid overlapping or excessive duplication of product offers to provide participants with balanced and diversified choices.

4. Pricing and Sales Regulations: Develop pricing and sales regulations to promote fair and transparent interactions between merchants and attendees. Encourage suppliers to clearly show all product pricing and offer information on acceptable payment options. Establish criteria for pricing consistency, price modifications, and any special promotions or discounts given throughout the event.

5. Booth Etiquette and Conduct: Establish booth etiquette and conduct guidelines in order to create a professional and respectful atmosphere for merchants and guests. Prohibit aggressive sales methods, harassment, and disruptive conduct that might distract from the overall craft fair experience. Encourage vendors to greet customers politely, participate in positive exchanges, and give useful information about their products without being aggressive or invasive.

6. Setup and Teardown Procedures: To ensure that the vendor process runs smoothly and efficiently, provide instructions and recommendations for set-up and tear-down. Specify load-in and load-out hours, parking arrangements, and other logistical specifics for accessing the event venue. Encourage vendors to come on schedule, use designated load-in and load-out locations, and follow any venue laws or restrictions.

7. Prioritize safety and accessibility issues for both vendors and attendees. Ensure that booth configurations adhere to fire rules, building restrictions, and other safety requirements. Provide instructions for handling hazardous items, electrical equipment, and other possible safety concerns. Ensure that the event site is accessible to all participants, including those with disabilities, and provide any necessary modifications.

8. Marketing and Promotion: Encourage merchants to actively participate in marketing and promotion campaigns leading up to the craft fair. Establish standards for advertising the event using social media, email marketing, word-of-mouth referrals, and other methods. Encourage vendors to publish event information, sneak peeks, and special deals with their networks to build interest and attract attendees.

9. Compliance with Laws and Regulations: Remind vendors to follow all necessary rules, regulations, and permissions regarding their participation in the craft fair. Provide information on sales tax requirements, food safety standards, licensing requirements, and any other legal duties that sellers must fulfill. Encourage vendors to get all required permissions and licenses ahead of time and verify that all items offered at the craft fair comply with applicable regulatory requirements.

10. Feedback and Communication: Create routes for vendors and organizers to address questions, issues, and feedback throughout the planning process and event. Encourage suppliers to offer feedback on their experiences, make suggestions for changes, and convey any concerns or obstacles they encounter in a timely way. Maintain open and honest communication to build a collaborative and supportive relationship between vendors and event organizers.

Creating clear and thorough vendor criteria may help organizers assure a well-organized, professional, and successful craft fair experience for vendors, guests, and organizers alike. These principles assist in ensuring uniformity, fairness, and quality standards while also providing a good and courteous atmosphere for all participants.

Handling Vendor Applications and Payments

Handling vendor applications and payments is an important component of organizing a craft fair since it requires managing the process of approving vendors and collecting money to cover expenditures and assure the fair's financial sustainability.

Here's an in-depth look at how to properly manage vendor applications and fees:

Streamline the application procedure for craft fair businesses: Create an online application form or vendor registration gateway where vendors may enter their information, product photographs, descriptions, price, and any other necessary information.

To ensure that the selection process is transparent and fair, clearly convey the application deadlines, requirements, and selection criteria to potential suppliers.

Review vendor applications carefully to determine product quality, originality, and appropriateness, as well as vendor professionalism and reputation. Consider variables such as product differentiation, workmanship, fit with the event concept, and market demand.

Acceptance and Notification: Promptly notify accepted suppliers when their applications are evaluated and approved. Provide clear directions for the following stages, such as booth assignment, payment information, and any further needs or documents.

Communicate cordially with vendors whose applications were not approved, offering constructive criticism if feasible and encouraging them to submit for future events. Establish clear and competitive booth costs that represent the value of participating in the craft fair while taking into account vendor budgets. Determine pricing structures depending on booth dimensions, location, amenities, and promotional possibilities.

Clearly define the payment procedure, timelines, and acceptable payment methods for merchants to submit booth fees. To suit vendor preferences, offer a variety of payment choices, such as online payment gateways, bank transfers, and checks. Set up a system for tracking and managing vendor payments, guaranteeing accurate record-keeping and timely fee processing. Send reminders to suppliers about future payment deadlines and immediately follow up on any outstanding payments.

Establish explicit procedures for booth fees, including cancellation, refund, and late payment penalties. Communicate these policies to vendors upfront to prevent misunderstandings and disputes. Provide standards for managing vendor refund claims, including what conditions will result in refunds and any related administrative costs or deductions. Consider things like event cancellation, vendor withdrawal, or unforeseen events beyond the vendor's control.

Ensure open and responsive contact with suppliers during the application and payment process. Respond to requests, offer help, and answer any issues or complaints from suppliers in a professional and timely manner.

Provide merchants with help and direction on logistics, booth setup, marketing tactics, and other elements of participation in the craft fair. Provide vendors with tools, information, and assistance to help them prepare for the event and achieve success. Organizers may attract high-quality vendors, minimize administrative work, and provide a favorable experience for craft fair vendors by creating a well-organized and clear approach for dealing with vendor applications and payments. Successful event planning requires effective communication, clear policies, and timely assistance.

Providing vendor support and help is critical to ensuring that craft fair merchants have a successful and happy experience. As organizers, it is critical to provide direction, resources, and assistance throughout the process, from the initial application stage to the event day itself.

Here's a full breakdown of how to provide successful vendor support and help:

Clear contact: Create clear channels of contact with vendors and ensure they have access to the information they require. Provide contact information for a designated point of contact or vendor liaison who can immediately respond to queries, issues, and requests for help. Keep vendors updated on critical deadlines, event updates, and any changes or developments relating to the craft show.

Provide vendors with information and support with the logistical aspects of participation in the craft fair, such as booth setup, load-in and load-out processes, parking arrangements, and venue access. Give vendors precise directions, maps, and diagrams to help them traverse the event area and set up their booths quickly. Address any logistical issues or specific requests mentioned by suppliers to guarantee a seamless and trouble-free experience.

Booth Setup Assistance: Assist merchants with booth setup to build appealing and compelling displays for their products. Provide advice, recommendations, and best practices for booth layout, product placement, signage, and décor to increase visual appeal and attract guests. Give merchants access to resources like tables, chairs, power, and other booth setup equipment, and make sure they have enough room and facilities to successfully present their items.

Marketing and Promotion: Help sellers promote their participation in the craft fair while increasing their visibility and exposure to attendees. Give vendors the chance to be showcased in event marketing materials like website listings, social media postings, email newsletters, and promotional brochures. Encourage merchants to use their own marketing platforms, such as social media, websites, and email lists, to promote their participation at the craft fair and increase traffic to their booths.

Sales and Customer Service: Provide vendors with direction and support on sales methods, customer service best practices, and strategies for optimizing sales prospects at the craft fair. Provide advice on how to engage guests, properly demonstrate items, and close sales in a professional manner. Address any issues or concerns voiced by vendors concerning sales transactions, prices, or consumer inquiries, and provide help as needed to ensure that visitors have a great shopping experience.

Networking chances: Provide chances for merchants to engage with one another, share experiences, and form partnerships within the artisan community. Organize vendor meet-and-greets, networking sessions, or online forums where merchants may share ideas, work together on joint marketing, and encourage one another. Create a collaborative and supportive atmosphere where suppliers may exchange thoughts, resources, and advice to help one another flourish.

Post-Event Follow-Up: Following the craft fair, contact vendors to get feedback on their experience, answer any post-event questions or concerns, and show gratitude for their participation. Conduct post-event surveys or interviews to gain insight on areas for improvement and suggestions for future events. Maintain continual communication with suppliers to keep them updated on forthcoming events, opportunities, and resources that may be of interest to them.

Providing comprehensive vendor support and assistance entails proactive communication, logistical guidance, marketing and promotion assistance, sales support, networking opportunities, and post-event follow-up to ensure vendors have a positive and successful experience at the craft fair. Providing committed assistance and resources allows organizers to build strong connections with vendors, improve the overall quality of the craft fair, and contribute to its long-term success.

Managing Vendor Relations

Managing vendor relations is an important component of arranging a craft fair since it entails developing and maintaining excellent relationships with merchants to assure their happiness, collaboration, and ongoing involvement in the event. Effective vendor relations management involves a variety of actions and techniques aimed at encouraging open communication, resolving vendor requirements and concerns, and building a friendly and collaborative atmosphere.

Here's a full breakdown of how to efficiently manage vendor relationships:

1. Communication: Ensure clear communication with vendors and keep in continuous touch during event preparation and execution. Provide suppliers with regular updates, information, and resources to keep them informed and involved. Encourage open discussion and feedback, and respond to vendor questions, comments, and concerns. Clear and effective communication promotes trust and openness in vendor partnerships.

2. Relationship Building: Develop positive ties with vendors. Take the time to get to know vendors personally, learn about their operations, and show real interest in their success. Developing rapport and trust with suppliers fosters a helpful and collaborative atmosphere in which they feel valued and appreciated. Attend vendor meet-and-greet events, networking seminars, or workshops to build contacts and partnerships.

3. Provide proactive support and help to vendors throughout the process, including registration and post-event follow-up. Provide advice, resources, and support with logistical issues such as booth setup, load-in and load-out processes, and venue access. Provide marketing and promotional assistance to suppliers to help them increase their exposure and sales chances. Address any concerns or obstacles in a timely and professional manner to demonstrate your dedication to vendor satisfaction.

4. Regularly analyze vendor needs and preferences to assure satisfaction and suggest areas for improvement. Conduct surveys, interviews, or feedback sessions to gain insight about vendor experiences, satisfaction levels, and ideas for improvement. Use vendor input to improve decision-making, procedures, and the overall vendor experience.

5. Conflict Resolution: Resolve issues with vendors in a fair and constructive manner. Listen to the vendor's concerns, acquire all necessary information, and attempt to identify mutually acceptable solutions. Approach dispute resolution with professionalism, sensitivity, and a commitment to maintaining healthy relationships. Establish clear standards and processes for dealing with vendor

complaints or grievances, and guarantee fast resolution to reduce interruptions to the craft fair.

6. Recognize and congratulate sellers for their efforts at the craft fair. Express your appreciation for their hard work, inventiveness, and commitment to making the event a success. Publicly acknowledge vendors through social media postings, website features, or event signage to emphasize their presence and products. Small acts of appreciation, such as thank-you cards or gifts of gratitude, may go a long way toward establishing goodwill and loyalty among vendors.

7. Long-Term Relationship Building: Build ties with suppliers beyond a single event. Cultivate regular contact and interaction with suppliers throughout the year to sustain relationships and keep them informed of potential prospects. Consider providing incentives or perks to returning exhibitors, such as preferred booth selection or reduced participation costs. Investing in long-term relationships with vendors promotes loyalty, trust, and collaboration, all of which contribute to the craft fair's overall success and sustainability.

Managing vendor relations entails proactive communication, relationship building, support and assistance, needs assessment, dispute resolution, acknowledgment and gratitude, and long-term relationship development. By prioritizing vendor happiness, cultivating strong relationships, and successfully resolving vendor

Event Execution and Operations

Event execution and operations are important components of running a successful craft show. This phase entails putting all of the planning and preparation into action so that the event goes successfully and meets its objectives.

Here's a thorough summary of event execution and operations:

Before the craft show begins, organizers must finish all essential preparations. This includes preparing the event space according to the planned layout and design. Organizers should work with suppliers to assign booth space, provide essential equipment and utilities, and handle any last-minute logistical concerns.

Additionally, organizers should add signage, decorations, and other visual components to enhance the overall mood and branding of the craft fair.

Vendor Check-In and Setup: On event day, merchants will check in and set up their booths. Organizers should provide a distinct check-in area so vendors may register, get booth assignments, and collect any event documents or instructions. Staff or volunteers should be ready to help exhibitors unload their wares, set up their displays, and answer any onsite problems or inquiries. Clear communication and effective coordination are required to enable a seamless check-in and setup procedure for vendors.

To create a successful craft fair, organizers must monitor different operational factors. This involves controlling event flow and traffic to avoid congestion and provide a pleasant experience for guests. Organizers should keep an eye on crowd numbers, modify signage or booth layouts as appropriate, and deal with any safety or logistical difficulties that occur. Furthermore, organizers must guarantee that amenities such as toilets, food vendors, and lounging places are well-maintained and easily accessible to guests.

Providing exceptional customer service is key to creating a great experience for guests and encouraging repeat participation in future events. Organizers should be present to answer questions, offer directions, and respond to any complaints or criticism from participants. Additionally, organizers might encourage visitor participation through interactive events, demonstrations, or workshops given by vendors. Encourage contact between merchants and consumers to create a lively and engaging atmosphere at the craft fair.

Managing sales transactions is a crucial component of event operations. Organizers should ensure that merchants have the tools and resources they need to accept payments, such as cash registers, card readers, or mobile payment devices. Organizers should give clear signs and instructions to show guests how to make purchases from exhibitors. Organizers may also consider providing a central checkout area or information booth where guests may get more information, make purchases, or get help with transactions.

Prioritize safety and emergency preparedness for guests, vendors, and personnel during the event. Organizers should have a complete emergency preparation plan in place, which includes methods for dealing with medical crises, evacuations, and other unexpected events. Organizers should educate staff and volunteers in emergency protocols and ensure they understand how to respond responsibly in the event of an emergency. Organizers should undertake frequent safety inspections during the event to detect and remedy any possible dangers or safety problems.

After the craft fair, organizers must manage cleanup and wrap-up to return the facility to its former state. This involves taking down booths, removing decorations and signs, and disposing of any garbage or debris. Organizers must collaborate with suppliers to ensure timely packing and removal of all items from the site. Organizers may also perform a post-event debriefing or review to collect feedback, analyze the event's success, and recommend areas for improvement in future events.

Event execution and management need meticulous preparation, organization, and attention to detail to provide a successful and memorable craft fair experience for all attendees, vendors, and organizers. Organizers can create a positive and engaging event that showcases the talents of local artisans and crafters by efficiently managing pre-event setup, vendor check-in and setup, event operations, customer service, sales and transactions, safety and emergency preparedness, and post-event cleanup and wrap-up.

Preparing For Event Day

Preparing for event day is an important phase in organizing a craft fair since it entails finalizing all logistical arrangements, working with vendors, and ensuring that everything is in order for a successful event.

Here's a thorough summary of the preparation process:

1. Location Setup: Organizers must guarantee the event location follows the planned layout and design. This may entail arranging tables, chairs, and other furniture, putting up signage and decorations, and keeping the site clean and appealing. Organizers should also ensure that utilities like power, water, and toilet facilities are operational and accessible to vendors and guests.

2. Vendor Coordination: Organizers should connect with vendors to confirm attendance and offer event specifics, such as load-in and load-out timings, booth allocations, and any special instructions or requirements. Vendors may require assistance with logistical preparations, such as parking or access to their booths, so organizers should be accessible to answer any questions or issues they may have.

3. Equipment and Supplies: Organizers must ensure all required equipment and supplies are present and operational for the craft show. This might include tables, chairs, tents or canopies, signs, lighting, and any other supplies required for vendor booths or event operations. Organizers should also have a backup plan in place to handle any equipment problems or last-minute supply requirements that may emerge.

4. Staff and Volunteers: Organizers should form a team of staff and volunteers to help with event operations. Assign defined tasks and duties to team members, such as vendor check-in, crowd control, customer service, and emergency response. Conduct a briefing or training session to ensure that all staff and volunteers are aware of their responsibilities and prepared to manage any situations that may occur during the event.

5. Safety and Security: Preserving the safety and security of vendors, guests, and event workers is crucial on event day. Organizers should do a comprehensive safety examination of the site to detect and resolve any possible dangers, such as uneven surfaces, trip hazards, or impediments. Additionally, organizers should have a strategy in place for dealing with crises or security problems, including processes for evacuations, medical emergencies, and calling authorities as needed.

6. Event Promotion: Organizers should market the craft fair in advance to increase attendance and participation. This might involve publishing on social media, sending out email newsletters, distributing brochures or posters across the neighborhood, and contacting local media outlets for coverage. Organizers should also urge merchants to publicize their participation in the craft fair via their own marketing channels in order to reach a larger audience.

7. Last inspections and rehearsals: Organizers should do last inspections in the days before the event to ensure everything is ready for the big day. This may entail checking event schedules, verifying vendor agreements, and walking through the site to handle any last-minute concerns. Organizers should also do rehearsals or run-throughs of important event processes, such as vendor check-in, crowd control, and emergency response, to ensure that staff and volunteers are ready and organized.

Organizers may ensure a smooth and successful craft fair experience for exhibitors, guests, and event personnel by properly planning for the event day and attending to all logistical issues. Effective planning enables event organizers to anticipate and manage potential obstacles, establish a friendly and orderly setting, and ensure that all attendees have a great and memorable experience.

Managing On-Site Operations

Managing on-site operations at a craft show is critical to maintaining a smooth and successful event. It entails managing all parts of event execution and dealing with any difficulties or obstacles that may develop on the day of the event. Here's a comprehensive overview of managing on-site operations.

Organizers must actively work with vendors during the event to meet their needs and address any on-site issues or requests. This involves aiding exhibitors with booth setup and teardown, resolving logistical concerns such as power outages or equipment failures, and responding to any last-minute demands. Organizers should keep open communication with vendors and be ready to help them during the event.

Effective crowd management ensures a great experience for both guests and merchants. Organizers should keep track of crowd sizes and change traffic flow as needed to avoid congestion and create a comfortable environment. This might include controlling foot circulation, adjusting signs or booth layouts, and deploying crowd control measures in high-traffic areas. Organizers should also be prepared to deal with any crowd-related issues or concerns that may develop throughout the event.

Providing good customer service is essential for generating a positive experience for attendees and vendors. Organizers should be available to answer questions, offer directions, and help participants with any requests or problems they may have. This includes resolving issues with event logistics, vendor merchandise, and general information about the craft fair. Organizers should maintain a cheerful and approachable manner while aiming to surpass participants' expectations for customer service.

Supporting merchants on the event day is crucial for their pleasure and success. Organizers should be present to help vendors with any on-site requirements or obstacles they may face, such as refilling supplies, resolving technological issues, or assisting with client engagement. Additionally, organizers should foster communication between vendors and event workers to promptly and effectively address any issues or requests.

The craft fair prioritizes safety and emergency preparedness to ensure a secure atmosphere. Organizers should be careful in recognizing and correcting any potential safety dangers or issues, such as tripping hazards, overcrowding, or blocked exits. Furthermore, organizers should have a full emergency preparation plan in place, which includes processes for dealing with medical crises, evacuations, and other unexpected situations. Organizers should educate their staff and volunteers in emergency protocols and ensure they are prepared to respond swiftly and efficiently to any situations that may occur.

Effective event flow and logistical management are crucial for a successful craft show. Organizers are responsible for several areas of event operations, including vendor check-in and setup, attendee registration, sales transactions, and overall event coordination. Organizers ensure that event personnel and volunteers complete their duties on time and handle any logistical issues that may arise during the event day through effective communication.

Managing on-site operations at a craft show involves strong collaboration, communication, and problem-solving abilities. Organizers may guarantee a successful and pleasurable event for all participants by managing vendor coordination, crowd control, customer service, vendor support, safety and emergency preparedness, and event flow and logistics.

Check-In Procedure Process

A seamless check-in procedure is critical for setting the correct tone and providing a great experience for merchants attending a craft fair. A well-organized and quick check-in procedure makes vendors feel welcome, prepared, and supported as soon as they arrive at the event.

Here's a full explanation of how to ensure a seamless check-in process:

To ensure a smooth check-in procedure, organizers should plan ahead of time for the craft fair. This includes developing a thorough check-in strategy that describes the stages, determining the check-in site, and preparing the relevant equipment and resources.

Organizers should also provide critical check-in information to vendors ahead of time, such as check-in timings, needed documents or paperwork, and specific instructions.

To lead merchants to the right place during the craft fair, organizers should clearly identify the check-in location. Clear and prominent signage allows vendors to readily identify the check-in location, reducing confusion and delays.

Organizers should utilize big, easy-to-read signage with clear directions and information to help vendors find their way. Design an effective and simplified check-in procedure to reduce wait times and ensure seamless operation.

To efficiently accommodate vendors, organizers should set up a specific check-in space with numerous check-in kiosks. Staff or volunteers should be present at each station to help merchants with the check-in process and to answer any questions or concerns that may arise.

To guarantee a smooth check-in procedure, organizers should have all relevant papers and supplies organized. This might contain vendor contracts, booth assignments, event maps, parking cards, and any other pertinent details. Organized paperwork speeds up the check-in process and ensures that merchants have all they need to set up their booths and participate in the artisan fair.

Staff that facilitate the check-in process should be polite, welcoming, and approachable. They should greet merchants with a smile, give clear directions, and offer help as required. Having polite and helpful personnel contributes to a favorable first impression and sets the tone for a successful and pleasurable craft fair event.

Effective communication is essential for a seamless check-in procedure. Organizers should provide critical information to vendors in advance, including check-in processes, needed documents, and any special instructions or needs.

During the check-in process, personnel should communicate effectively with vendors, offer updates on wait times or delays, and respond to any queries or complaints quickly.

Problem Resolution:

Even with careful planning, complications or obstacles may develop throughout the check-in procedure. Organizers should be ready to manage these circumstances swiftly and efficiently in order to prevent disruptions and keep the check-in process operating smoothly.

This might include debugging technological difficulties, resolving disagreements or inconsistencies, and offering alternate solutions as needed.

Establishing a successful check-in process needs meticulous preparation, clear communication, and effective implementation. Organizers may establish a great and stress-free check-in experience for craft fair exhibitors by planning ahead of time, providing clear signs, keeping an organized check-in area, greeting merchants with courteous personnel, and swiftly addressing any concerns that arise.

Handling Emergencies

Handling emergencies and contingencies is an important component of event preparation, especially craft fairs, since unanticipated circumstances may happen that need a prompt and effective reaction to protect the safety and well-being of guests, vendors, and personnel.

Here's a full breakdown of how to manage crises and eventualities during a craft fair:

Preparation is crucial when dealing with crises and disasters. Organizers should create a complete emergency plan, including procedures for a variety of situations, such as medical emergencies, extreme weather occurrences, fires, security concerns, and other potential catastrophes. The plan should contain clearly defined roles and duties for event personnel and volunteers, designated emergency exits and assembly locations, emergency service contact information, and communication and coordination processes.

Organizers should train and educate all event personnel and volunteers on emergency protocols and duties. Before the craft fair, organizers may hold training sessions or workshops to review emergency protocols, practice evacuation methods, and familiarize workers with the locations of emergency equipment such as fire extinguishers, first aid kits, and AEDs (automated external defibrillators).

Effective communication is crucial during emergencies to keep stakeholders informed and aware of the situation. Organizers should develop communication channels for sharing information with event workers, vendors, attendees, and emergency services.

During an emergency, organizers can convey vital instructions and updates through various communication techniques, such as public address announcements, mobile messaging, social media updates, and location signs.

During an emergency, organizers should stay cool and adhere to the set strategy. This might include beginning evacuation protocols, guiding guests and vendors to designated emergency exits and assembly places, and working with emergency services as needed. Organizers should also be prepared to help those with impairments or special needs so that everyone may securely leave the premises.

Organizers should create processes to coordinate with local authorities and emergency services during severe emergencies or crises. This might include contacting emergency services such as police, fire, and medical professionals to request assistance, giving them pertinent information about the issue, and following their orders and suggestions to ensure a coordinated response.

After an emergency, organizers should offer support and help to impacted people as needed. This may involve giving first aid or medical help, facilitating access to counseling or support services, and assisting in the reunification of separated parties.

Organizers should also hold a post-incident debriefing to assess the reaction to the situation, identify areas for improvement, and adopt corrective steps to improve emergency preparation for future events.

Resolving crises and eventualities at a craft fair needs careful preparation, efficient communication, and quick action to protect the safety and well-being of all attendees. Organizers can effectively manage emergencies and contingencies and ensure the craft fair's success and safety by preparing, training staff and volunteers, establishing clear communication protocols, implementing effective emergency response procedures, coordinating with authorities, and providing post-emergency support.

Performance Input and Assessment Approach

Collecting input and assessing performance are critical steps in enhancing and refining the craft fair experience for both merchants and guests.

Here's a thorough look at how organizers may efficiently gather feedback and evaluate performance:

Feedback Collection: Organizers can gather feedback from craft fair stakeholders such as vendors, attendees, staff, volunteers, and sponsors. Organizers can collect feedback through various mechanisms, such as surveys, feedback forms, direct interactions, and internet reviews. Participants can provide thorough feedback on their experiences by submitting surveys and feedback forms electronically or in person.

Organizers should collect feedback at critical moments before, during, and after the craft expo. Before the event, organizers can collect input from vendors throughout the registration process to better understand their expectations and preferences. During the event, organizers can collect real-time feedback from participants via on-site questionnaires or interactive feedback kiosks. After the event, organizers can contact vendors and participants to get detailed feedback on their entire experience.

Stakeholder feedback can cover various topics, such as product quality, event layout, offerings, customer service, marketing effectiveness, and areas for improvement. To acquire a thorough knowledge of the craft fair experience, organizers should solicit both quantitative data (such as ratings or rankings) and qualitative input (such as comments or suggestions).

After collecting feedback, organizers should examine the data for trends, patterns, and insights. This might include sorting input into various themes or issues, collecting numeric ratings or scores, and synthesizing qualitative remarks to uncover common themes or areas for improvement. Organizers might utilize data analysis tools or software to speed up the process and extract valuable insights from feedback data.

To evaluate the craft fair's performance, organizers should use set metrics and targets in addition to gathering feedback. Attendance counts, sales figures, vendor satisfaction ratings, guest satisfaction ratings, sponsor return on investment (ROI), and other key performance indicators (KPIs) pertinent to the craft fair's aims are all examples of performance metrics. By comparing actual performance to specified goals and standards, organizers may evaluate the craft fair's success and find areas for future development. Organizers may use feedback and performance evaluations to uncover actionable insights and recommendations for future craft fairs. This may include implementing specific changes or improvements based on vendor and attendee feedback, adjusting event logistics or operations to address identified issues, fine-tuning marketing and promotion strategies to better reach target audiences, and generally improving the craft fair experience for all participants.

Continuous improvement involves gathering feedback and evaluating performance to influence future craft shows. Organizers should incorporate comments and insights from previous events into future event planning and execution, with the goal of constantly improving the craft fair's quality, value, and overall experience for vendors, consumers, and other stakeholders.

Financial Management

Financial management is critical to the effective organization and operation of a craft show. It entails meticulous planning, budgeting, tracking spending and earnings, and ensuring financial viability throughout the event's lifespan.

Here's an in-depth look at financial management for beginning a craft fair:

To handle finances effectively, start by preparing a detailed budget for the craft show. This includes calculating all projected expenses, such as venue rental, permits and licenses, equipment rentals, marketing and promotion charges, staff and volunteer expenses, insurance premiums, and any other operational costs. Organizers should also predict prospective income sources, such as vendor fees, sponsorship money, ticket sales, and goods sales, to establish the craft fair's overall financial sustainability. To stay under budget, organizers must continuously monitor and limit expenditures after establishing one.

This may include negotiating advantageous terms with vendors and suppliers, exploring cost-effective solutions for event logistics and operations, and applying cost-cutting measures wherever possible without sacrificing event quality.

Organizers should also be prepared to make budget adjustments as needed in response to changing conditions or unanticipated expenditures that may develop during the craft fair's planning and execution phases. To ensure the craft fair's financial success, organizers should aggressively explore and optimize income sources, in addition to limiting expenditures. This could include diversifying revenue streams by offering different sponsorship packages, selling booth spaces to vendors, selling tickets or admission passes to attendees, and providing additional revenue-generating opportunities like food and beverage sales, merchandise sales, or onsite activities and attractions.

Organizers should deliberately price various income sources in order to maximize profit while remaining competitive in the market. To design and execute a successful craft fair, organizers must keep precise financial records and track all costs and earnings. Keep thorough records of all transactions, invoices, receipts, and financial paperwork, and reconcile accounts on a regular basis to verify their correctness. Organizers should also generate financial records and disclosures to give transparency and accountability to stakeholders like suppliers, sponsors, and financing partners, as well as to inform and build fair decision-making processes.

Effective cash flow management ensures the craft fair's financial stability and sustainability. Organizers must carefully manage cash inflows and outflows to provide enough liquidity during the event's lifespan. Organizers must establish payment terms with vendors and suppliers consistent with the craft fair's cash flow projections, monitor accounts receivable and payable, and implement cash flow optimization strategies, such as collecting vendor fees and sponsorships in advance and deferring certain expenses until revenues are realized.

Organizers must identify and manage financial risks while arranging a craft show. Budget overruns, income deficits, unforeseen costs, and economic downturns are all potential hazards to the event's financial sustainability. Organizers should create contingency plans and risk mitigation techniques to meet potential financial concerns, such as obtaining insurance, setting up emergency reserves, or diversifying revenue streams to lessen reliance on a single source of income.

Starting a craft fair requires effective financial management to ensure long-term success and sustainability. This entails balancing expenditures and revenues in order to create a favorable financial outcome for each iteration of the craft fair and lay a solid financial basis for subsequent events.

Budgeting For Start-Up

Budgeting for start-up costs is an important phase in the process of creating a craft fair since it provides the framework for financial planning and guarantees that the event is financially viable. Start-up costs are the first expenses involved in preparing for and arranging the craft show before it takes place.

Here's an in-depth look at budgeting for startup costs:

1. Venue rental is a big start-up cost for artisan fairs. Organizers must budget for the event venue rental charge, which might vary depending on location, size, amenities, and event duration. It is critical to explore and evaluate several venue possibilities to select one that falls within your budget while also meeting the event's criteria.

2. Permits and Licenses: Obtaining permits and licenses is an important start-up expenditure for craft fairs. This may include event operating permits, health and safety permits, food service permits (if available), and any other licenses mandated by municipal legislation. Organizers should budget for the application fees required to secure these permissions and ensure compliance with all legal criteria.

3. Marketing and Promotion: Investing in marketing and promotion is essential for increasing awareness and recruiting merchants and guests to the craft fair. This might include the costs of creating and producing promotional items like flyers, posters, and banners, as well as digital marketing expenses like social media advertising, email marketing, and website creation. Organizers may also budget for promotional events and cooperation with local companies or groups.

4. Equipment and Supplies: Organizers need to budget for renting or purchasing necessary equipment and supplies for the craft fair. Outdoor events may require tents or canopies, vendor booth tables and chairs, signs, lighting, sound equipment, and other event necessities. Organizers should also budget for supplies such as cleaning products, garbage cans, and toilet facilities to provide a comfortable and functioning event atmosphere.

5. Budget for Staff and Volunteer Expenses: Organizing and administering the craft show requires enough help from staff and volunteers. This may include the expenditures associated with employing event planners, security officers, parking attendants, and administrative staff. Organizers may also budget for costs associated with recruiting and training volunteers to help with different areas of the event, such as registration, crowd management, and customer service.

6. Insurance costs: Organizers should budget for insurance costs to cover any liabilities involved with conducting a craft show. This may include general liability insurance, event cancellation insurance, property insurance, and worker's compensation coverage for event workers and volunteers. The cost of insurance premiums might vary based on the size and scope of the event, the number of guests, and the type of coverage required.

7. Budget for administrative expenses to cover the operational costs of conducting the craft show. This may include charges for office supplies, communication (e.g., phone, internet), transportation, and professional services (e.g., legal, accounting). Organizers should carefully assess their administrative requirements and invest money accordingly to guarantee seamless and efficient event preparation and execution.

8. Contingency Fund: Budget for unforeseen costs or crises during craft show preparation and implementation. The contingency fund acts as a buffer against unanticipated obstacles or changes in conditions, ensuring that the event runs well and without compromising the budget. Organizers should set aside a proportion of the entire budget as a contingency fund to provide flexibility and financial stability during the event's lifespan.

Pricing

Setting pricing and fees for a craft fair requires careful consideration of a variety of criteria to ensure that the event is financially viable while also providing value to exhibitors and consumers.

Here's a full explanation of how to determine pricing and fees for a craft fair:

Craft fairs rely heavily on vendor booth fees to generate money. When calculating booth prices, organizers should consider the size and placement of the booth, the facilities supplied (e.g., tables, chairs, power), the length of the event, and the projected foot traffic. Booth prices should be competitive in the market while covering event-related expenditures such as venue rental, permits, marketing, personnel, and other operational expenses.

Organizers may provide early-bird discounts or promotions to encourage vendor sign-ups and secure booth spots. Early bird discounts often include giving a lower booth price to vendors that register and pay by a certain date. This allows organizers to measure early interest in the craft fair, generate income up front, and encourage merchants to commit to participating in the event.

Organizers may provide additional services or add-ons to vendors for an additional price. For example, organizers may charge a higher cost for premium booth placements, give access to power or Wi-Fi for an extra fee, or offer marketing and promotional packages to assist exhibitors in increasing their exposure and sales during the event. Vendors who choose to buy these extra services should expect them to be reasonably priced and deliver actual benefit.

Some craft fairs may require guests to pay an entry fee to enter the event. Admission fees can help event organizers cover costs and create additional cash. When selecting entry rates, organizers should consider the target demographic, the perceived value of the event, market competition, and attendees' affordability.

To make the event more inclusive and accessible, organizers may give cheap or free entrance to specific groups, such as children, the elderly, or military members. Organizers can make cash through sponsorship by working with businesses, organizations, or people that support the craft fair. Sponsorship packages may offer a variety of perks, including logo placement on promotional materials, event booth space, mentions in marketing materials and announcements, and more promotional possibilities. Price sponsorship packages based on the visibility and publicity sponsors receive, as well as the perceived value of the sponsorship advantages.

Organizers should create clear payment terms and regulations for suppliers, sponsors, and attendees to enable seamless financial transactions and prevent disagreements. Payment conditions may include deadlines for submitting booth fees or sponsorship payments, approved payment methods (such as credit card, check, or online payment), and refund procedures in the event of cancellations or adjustments. Clear communication of payment terms and rules reduces misunderstandings and guarantees compliance by all parties involved.

To determine pricing and fees for a craft fair, organizers should do market research and competitive analysis to identify industry trends and benchmark against similar events. This assists organizers in determining the best pricing approach that strikes a balance between competitiveness and profitability, ensuring that the craft fair benefits both merchants and attendees.

Determining pricing and fees for a craft fair requires a strategic approach that takes into account factors such as vendor booth fees, early bird discounts, additional services and add-ons, admission fees for attendees, sponsorship opportunities, payment terms and policies, market research, and competitor analysis. By carefully analyzing these aspects, organizers may set pricing and levies that ensure the craft fair's financial viability while also delivering value to participants and stakeholders.

Income and Cost Tracking

Tracking income and costs is an important part of financial management when beginning a craft fair. All event-related income and expenditures are recorded, monitored, and analyzed to ensure financial transparency, accountability, and sustainability.

Here's a full explanation of how to manage sales and costs during a craft fair:

Proper records of all income generated from the craft fair should be kept by organizers. This includes revenue streams such as vendor booth fees, sponsorship payments, ticket sales, item sales, concessions, and any other event-related money. Document each revenue transaction in a timely and accurate manner, including the date, amount, payer information, and payment purpose.

Organizers should manage and report all expenditures related to arranging and administering the craft show. This comprises venue rental fees, permits and licenses, marketing and promotional charges, equipment rentals, staff and volunteer expenses, insurance premiums, administrative costs, and any other event-related operational expenses. To make monitoring and analysis easier, organizers should classify costs in a methodical manner.

Organizers must account for any in-kind gifts or donations received during the craft fair, in addition to monetary transactions. This might include donations of products or services from sponsors, suppliers, volunteers, or other stakeholders. Report in-kind donations as income or offset them by associated costs in the financial records, valuing them at fair market value.

Organizers should keep orderly and current financial records to efficiently manage revenue and costs. This might include utilizing accounting software or spreadsheets to record transactions, classify costs, reconcile accounts, and create financial reports. One should maintain financial data securely and in a manner that is easy to access and retrieve for auditing or reporting.

Ensure accuracy by reconciling bank statements with financial records on a regular basis. Compare the transactions recorded in the financial records to the transactions shown on the bank statement to ensure proper accounting of all revenue and expenses. Address and remedy any inconsistencies in the financial records as soon as possible to maintain accuracy.

Analyzing Financial Performance: After tracking income and costs, organizers should examine the craft fair's profitability and sustainability. This might include comparing actual revenue and costs to anticipated levels, calculating important financial ratios and indicators such as gross profit margin, net profit margin, return on investment (ROI), and break-even analysis, and finding areas for improvement or cost-cutting options. Organizers should undertake variance analysis to uncover substantial disparities between actual and budgeted financial outcomes. Positive variances (when actual revenue exceeds budgeted revenue or actual expenses are less than budgeted expenses) may indicate financial success or opportunities for additional investment, whereas negative variances (when actual revenue falls short of budgeted revenue or actual expenses exceed budgeted expenses) may highlight areas for improvement or cost-cutting measures.

Financial Reporting: Organizers should disseminate financial reports to stakeholders, including suppliers, sponsors, financing partners, and internal stakeholders (e.g., organizing committee members and the board of directors). Financial reports should give a clear and complete picture of the craft fair's financial performance, including a review of income and costs, budget variation analysis, important financial metrics, and any other pertinent information. Transparent and timely financial reporting fosters confidence and responsibility among stakeholders while also facilitating informed decision-making.

Handling Payments and Transactions

Handling payments and transactions is an important part of running a craft fair since it includes collecting fees from merchants, processing ticket sales from guests, managing sponsor contributions, and handling different financial transactions linked to the event.

Here's a full explanation of how to manage money and transactions at a craft fair:

1. Payment Methods: Organizers should provide a variety of payment options to meet the needs of vendors, participants, and sponsors. Credit/debit cards, checks, cash, and online payment systems like PayPal or Stripe are all examples of common payment methods. By offering a choice of payment alternatives, organizers may make it easier for participants to complete transactions and reduce obstacles to participation.

2. Vendor Booth Fees: Organizers should provide clear payment conditions and deadlines to participating businesses. This may include establishing fee payment dates, designating acceptable payment methods, and explaining any penalties or late fees for late payments. Organizers should also send invoices or receipts to suppliers after payment to document the transaction and guarantee transparency.

3. Ticket Sales: Organizers of events with entrance costs should have effective ticket sales systems. This might include employing online ticketing systems, selling tickets in advance via the event website or specified ticket shops, and selling tickets on-site at the craft fair. Organizers must ensure that ticket pricing is properly disclosed to guests and that ticket sales are carefully documented in order to assess attendance and income.

4. Sponsor Contributions: Organizers should create clear payment conditions and agreements with sponsors for financial contributions to the craft show. This may involve identifying the cost of sponsorship, describing the benefits or perks of sponsorship packages, and establishing sponsorship payment dates. After receiving payment, organizers should provide sponsors with invoices or receipts to authenticate the transaction and preserve openness.

5. Handling Cash Transactions: Organizers should establish security and accuracy procedures for cash payments. This may involve designating authorized cashiers or payment booths to handle cash transactions, implementing safe cash handling procedures and protocols, and reconciling cash receipts on a regular basis to ensure accuracy and discover any anomalies.

6. Online Payment Processing: Organizers should use secure and dependable payment solutions to protect sensitive financial information during online transactions. This might include using trusted payment gateways or third-party platforms that adhere to industry data security and encryption requirements. Organizers should also offer attendees clear information on how to make safe online payments.

7. Refund rules: Organizers should set clear refund rules for vendor booth fees, ticket sales, and sponsor contributions to handle cancellations, adjustments, or disputes. Organizers should specify the conditions under which they issue refunds, any related fees or penalties, and the procedure for requesting and processing returns in their refund policies. Organizers should disclose refund terms to participants in advance to manage expectations and avoid misunderstandings.

8. Financial Reconciliation: Organizers of craft fairs should undertake frequent financial reconciliation to guarantee accurate and transparent management of payments and transactions. Organizers of craft fairs should compare recorded transactions to actual payments received, reconcile bank records, and resolve any anomalies or errors. Financial reconciliation maintains the integrity of financial records and ensures proper handling of payments and transactions.

Managing payments and transactions at a craft fair entails establishing clear payment terms, providing multiple payment methods, processing vendor booth fees, ticket sales, and sponsor contributions, securely handling cash transactions, implementing online payment processing systems, establishing refund policies, and performing regular financial reconciliation. Organizers may maintain financial transparency, security, and efficiency at the craft fair by adhering to best practices in payment and transaction processing.

Evaluating Financial Performance

Evaluating financial performance is critical for craft fair organizers to determine the event's profitability and sustainability. It entails examining several financial data and indicators to determine the profitability, efficiency, and general health of the craft fair's finances.

Here's a full summary of how to assess financial performance at a craft fair:

Organizers should assess all revenue streams from the craft fair, such as vendor booth fees, ticket sales, sponsor contributions, retail sales, snacks, and more. By comparing actual revenue to planned revenue and prior event revenues, organizers may determine if the craft fair accomplished its revenue objectives and suggest areas for development or growth in future events.

Expense Analysis: Organizers should assess overall expenses for arranging and managing the craft show. This includes payments for venue rents, permits, and licenses; marketing and promotional charges; equipment rentals; staff and volunteer expenses; insurance premiums; administrative costs; and any other operational expenses. By comparing actual expenditures to anticipated expenses and prior event expenses, organizers may assess cost effectiveness, identify areas of overspending or inefficiency, and apply cost-cutting initiatives for future events.

To analyze profitability, organizers should deduct expenditures from income to determine the net profit or loss from the craft show. Positive net profit suggests that the craft fair made more income than it spent on expenditures, while negative net profit shows that expenses surpassed revenue. By measuring profitability, organizers may analyze the craft fair's financial feasibility and performance, as well as decide whether changes are required to boost profitability in future events.

Organizers should determine the gross profit margin, which is the proportion of sales over the cost of goods sold (COGS). To compute the gross profit margin, organizers divide the gross profit (revenue less COGS) by total revenue and multiply by 100.

A larger gross profit margin signifies increased profitability and efficiency in producing revenue in comparison to the cost of products sold. Organizers should calculate the net profit margin by subtracting expenses like COGS, operating costs, and taxes from income. To determine the net profit margin, divide the net profit by total sales and multiply the result by 100. Managing expenditures more efficiently in relation to income results in a larger net profit margin.

Organizers should compute the return on investment (ROI) to evaluate the effectiveness of their investment in staging the craft fair. To calculate ROI, divide net profit by total investment (including all event-related expenditures) and multiply by 100. A greater ROI signifies a better return on investment for the craft fair, proving the event's financial success and efficacy.

To examine the financial flow of a craft fair, organizers should track cash input and outflow during event planning and execution. Positive cash flow suggests that the craft fair earned more money than it spent, while negative cash flow shows that cash outflows outweighed cash inflows. Cash flow analysis allows organizers to examine the craft fair's liquidity and financial health, ensuring that there is enough cash on hand to pay expenditures and satisfy financial commitments.

Organizers can evaluate the craft fair's financial performance using various ratios, including liquidity (e.g., current ratio, quick ratio), efficiency (e.g., inventory turnover, accounts receivable turnover), and leverage (e.g., debt-to-equity ratio, interest coverage ratio). These ratios provide valuable insights into various aspects of the craft fair's financial performance, helping organizers identify strengths and weaknesses that require attention or improvement.

Analyzing sales, costs, profitability, cash flow, financial ratios, and other indicators may help organizers evaluate the craft fair's overall financial health and success. This comprehensive review assists organizers in identifying areas of success and development, making educated decisions regarding future events, and developing strategies to increase the craft fair's financial sustainability and profitability.

Evaluating financial performance for a craft fair entails examining a variety of financial measures and indicators, such as revenue, costs, profitability, gross profit margin, net profit margin, ROI, cash flow, financial ratios, and overall financial health. By completing a thorough review of financial performance, organizers may analyze the craft fair's success and sustainability, identify areas for development, and make educated decisions to improve future financial outcomes.

Growth and Expansion Strategies for Starting a Craft Fair

Craft fairs, like any other business, may benefit from strategic development and expansion strategies to broaden their reach, influence, and financial viability over time.

Here is a full summary of development and expansion options for beginning a craft fair:

Before executing growth plans, organizers should perform market research and analysis to find expansion prospects and understand the changing demands and preferences of their target audience. This might include studying market trends, competition data, polling potential participants and attendees, and obtaining feedback from previous events to influence decision-making.

Craft fairs can expand their offerings by introducing new features, activities, or themes to attract a wider audience. This might feature live music performances, interactive seminars or demonstrations, food and beverage options, children's activities, or themed zones focused on certain craft categories or artisanal items. Diversification may bring in new customers and merchants while improving the overall experience and value proposition of the craft show.

Expanding into new markets may help craft fair organizers reach new audiences and enhance participation. This might include creating satellite events in nearby towns or regions, collaborating with local community organizations or business associations, or focusing on certain demographic groups like families, millennials, and seniors. Expanding into new areas allows organizers to broaden their participation base and make more cash.

Craft fairs might benefit from collaboration and partnerships with other organizations, corporations, or community groups to expand their reach. This might entail developing strategic alliances with local craftsmen, craft guilds, art galleries, or cultural groups to co-host or co-promote the event, utilizing their networks and resources to reach a larger audience. Collaborations with sponsors, vendors, and local companies may also lead to cross-promotion, cooperative marketing efforts, and pooled resources, all of which can help the craft fair succeed.

Expanding the craft fair's online presence and utilizing digital marketing platforms helps attract attendees from outside the local region. This might include developing a user-friendly website with event information, connecting with followers on social networking platforms, initiating targeted online advertising campaigns, and using email marketing to contact potential attendees and vendors.

An active internet presence may boost awareness, generate ticket sales, and make vendor recruiting easier for the craft fair. Obtaining sponsorship and financing from corporate sponsors, local companies, government agencies, or charitable groups can help support development and expansion activities. Organizers can approach potential sponsors with personalized sponsorship packages that include branding possibilities, promotional exposure, and other perks in return for financial assistance. Sponsorship can help to defray event expenses, support growth initiatives, and improve the overall quality and scale of the artisan fair.

Organizers should gather input from participants, sponsors, and stakeholders to evaluate growth methods and suggest areas for improvement. Organizers may iteratively enhance the craft fair experience, handle changing market demands, and maintain long-term development and success by listening to feedback, evaluating event data, and always improving their strategy.

Getting Feedback

Assessing the effectiveness of a craft fair and getting feedback from participants, attendees, vendors, sponsors, and other stakeholders is critical for organizers in understanding the event's strengths and flaws and identifying areas for improvement.

Here's a full breakdown of how to evaluate event success and get feedback:

1. Gather Attendee Input: Organizers can collect input from attendees through numerous means, such as online surveys, on-site questionnaires, social media polls, and direct encounters during the event. Attendee feedback may include general satisfaction with the event, the quality and diversity of craft sellers, price and affordability, accessibility, cleanliness, facilities, entertainment choices, and ideas for improvements. Organizers should review guest comments to find patterns, recurring themes, and areas for concern or appreciation. Positive comments can serve to reinforce the event's successful components, while constructive criticism can guide future planning and decisions.

2. Gathering feedback from craft sellers helps organizers understand their experiences, happiness, and recommendations for improvement. Organizers can send vendor questionnaires before, during, and after the event to collect input on topics such as booth

arrangement and layout, foot traffic and sales, organizer communication and support, logistics and operations, and overall event satisfaction. Vendor feedback gives essential insights into the vendor experience, any issues they may have faced, and possibilities for organizers to improve the vendor experience and recruit excellent suppliers in the future.

3. Gather Sponsor Input: Organizers should request input from sponsors to assess event satisfaction and ROI. Organizers might conduct sponsor surveys or arrange post-event meetings with sponsors to discuss their objectives, expectations, and feedback on how well the event met their marketing and branding goals. Sponsor feedback enables organizers to better understand sponsors' viewpoints, evaluate the success of sponsorship packages, and identify areas for improvement in order to attract and retain sponsors for future events.

4. Volunteer input: Volunteers are vital to the success of a craft fair, and their input may give significant insights into event operations and volunteer experiences. Organizers can solicit feedback from volunteers via post-event questionnaires, debrief sessions, or one-on-one interviews to assess their happiness, experience, issues, and recommendations for improvements. Volunteer feedback allows organizers to assess the efficacy of volunteer recruiting, training,

and support procedures, as well as make changes to improve the volunteer experience and retention for future events.

5. Data Analysis: Organizers should examine quantitative data, including attendance, income, vendor sales, ticket sales, and other key performance indicators (KPIs). Data analysis enables event organizers to assess the event's success against specified goals and benchmarks, uncover trends and patterns, and make data-driven decisions to enhance future events.

6. Stakeholder sessions: Organizers can host post-event debrief sessions with important stakeholders, such as organizing committee members, board members, and partners, to discuss event outcomes, analyze comments, and develop suggestions for improvements. Stakeholder meetings allow for open communication, cooperation, and decision-making to address issues and make changes based on input and data analysis.

Evaluating event success and soliciting feedback from attendees, vendors, sponsors, volunteers, and other stakeholders is critical for organizers to understand the craft fair's strengths and weaknesses, identify areas for improvement, and make informed decisions to improve the event's overall quality and impact. Organizers may assure the craft fair's long-term success and sustainability by gathering and evaluating input from diverse sources and incorporating stakeholders' opinions into the planning process.

Identifying Expansion Prospects

Identifying expansion prospects is critical to a craft fair's long-term success and sustainability.

Here's a comprehensive look at how organizers might find these opportunities:

Conduct market research and analysis to understand the present state of craft fairs and artisanal marketplaces. Determine trends in consumer tastes, craft industry advancements, and developing markets. Analyze demographic data to identify target audience attributes and preferences. Understanding market dynamics allows organizers to find niche markets, underserved sectors, and emerging trends that offer potential for expansion.

Gather comments from guests, merchants, sponsors, and stakeholders to identify the craft fair's strengths and flaws. Analyze comments to find areas for improvement and development potential. Look for reoccurring themes, ideas, and areas of unhappiness that can help shape future planning and growth efforts. Pay attention to feedback on the range of crafts available, price, amenities, entertainment, and overall experience to discover areas for improvement.

Explore partnership options with organizations, companies, and community groups to increase the craft fair's reach and effect. Collaboration with local craftsmen, craft guilds, art galleries, and cultural groups can increase the event's appeal and attract new attendees. Seek out collaborations with local companies for sponsorship, promotional assistance, and cross-promotion. Collaborations can help raise exposure, attract more participants, and improve the entire experience at the craft show.

Consider broadening the craft fair's offerings to attract new audiences and adapt to changing consumer tastes. Introduce new features, activities, or themes that appeal to a variety of interests and demographics. Include aspects like live music, interactive workshops, artisanal food and beverage options, children's activities, and themed zones dedicated to various craft categories. Diversification may attract a broader spectrum of consumers and merchants, boost income sources, and set the craft show apart from competition.

Expanding into new markets can help reach underserved populations. Consider creating satellite events in other towns or areas to broaden the scope of the craft fair. Target certain demographic groups, such as families, millennials, or the elderly, with marketing and programming tailored to their interests and preferences. Expansion into new areas may raise brand awareness, attract new customers, and boost income.

Develop novel marketing techniques to promote the craft show and attract new consumers. Investigate digital marketing platforms such as social media, email marketing, influencer collaborations, and online advertising to broaden the event's reach and engage prospective attendees. Use innovative content marketing strategies like storytelling, user-generated material, and immersive experiences to increase enthusiasm and interest in the craft show. Embracing creativity and innovation in marketing activities enables organizers to reach a larger audience and promote growth.

Consider implementing sustainability activities into your craft fair to attract environmentally concerned customers and stand out in the market. Implement eco-friendly activities such as waste reduction, recycling programs, energy-efficient operations, and encouraging vendors to use sustainable goods and practices. Highlighting the craft fair's dedication to sustainability may attract a socially conscious audience and improve the event's image, resulting in higher attendance and growth.

Expanding a Craft Fair

Expanding a craft fair to various sites is a strategic move that demands meticulous preparation, organization, and execution. Here's a thorough look at how organizers might effectively expand their craft fair to various locations:

Conduct rigorous market research to discover possible growth areas. Consider population demographics, customer preferences, competition, and the availability of appropriate venues. Evaluate the demand for artisanal items and crafts in each prospective location to determine the feasibility of expanding the craft fair to numerous places.

Create a detailed strategic plan outlining goals, objectives, and timelines for growing the craft fair to additional sites. Define the target markets for expansion, define criteria for picking additional locations, and develop an expansion plan. Consider the logistical, personnel, finance, marketing, and operational needs for each additional site.

Identify and acquire appropriate venues for the craft fair in each target area. Consider aspects including venue size, accessibility, amenities, parking availability, and price. Consider collaborating with local event venues, convention halls, parks, or community centers to hold the craft fair in many locations. Make sure that the venues you choose are appropriate for the craft fair's brand image and target demographic. Create a thorough logistics and operations strategy to ensure the craft show runs well across various venues. Coordinate transportation and logistics for suppliers, exhibitors, and visitors visiting each venue.

Create operational procedures for setup, teardown, registration, security, and client service at each location. Use technological solutions like event management software and communication tools to simplify operations across various sites. Manage vendor rosters for each craft fair site to ensure diversity and quality. Create vendor recruiting tactics to attract craftsmen, crafters, and makers in each local community. Support and assist vendors with the application process, booth setup, and event logistics.

Develop solid ties with merchants to ensure their pleasure and participation in the craft fair expansion. Develop specific marketing and promotion methods to increase awareness and enthusiasm for the craft fair at each venue. Customize marketing messaging and methods to reflect the distinct qualities and interests of the local community in each target area. To attract potential attendees and vendors, use a combination of online and offline marketing methods, including social media, email marketing, print advertising, local media partnerships, and community engagement.

Engage with local communities in each target area to foster relationships and a sense of belonging during the craft fair. Collaborate with local companies, organizations, and community leaders to publicize the event and encourage participation. Participate in local events, festivals, and community meetings to increase awareness and build relationships with the community. Include elements of local culture, customs, and interests in the craft fair programming to appeal to attendees and sellers at each site.

Continuous improvement involves evaluating and refining craft fair growth strategies based on feedback, data analysis, and lessons gained from each site. Collect input from attendees, vendors, sponsors, and other stakeholders to identify areas for improvement and handle any obstacles or concerns that may occur. Implement improvements and upgrades to the growth plan as needed to improve the craft fair's performance and success in many locations.

Growing a craft fair at many sites needs extensive market research, strategic planning, venue selection, logistics and operations management, vendor recruiting and management, marketing and promotion, community participation, and continual development. By taking a holistic approach and using local resources and connections, organizers may effectively extend their craft fair to numerous sites while providing distinctive experiences for guests and merchants in each region.

Create a Detailed Financial Strategy

Create a detailed financial strategy and budget to grow the artisan fair to numerous venues. Estimate the costs of venue rental, personnel, marketing and promotion, logistics, vendor recruiting, insurance, permits, and other fees for each site. Allocate resources and cash wisely to secure adequate funding for all parts of growth. To keep within budgetary restrictions and accomplish the intended results, regularly monitor spending and change the budget as necessary.

Risk management involves identifying and mitigating potential risks and problems while growing a craft show at numerous sites. Consider severe weather, site availability, competition from other events, logistical challenges, and financial uncertainty. Create backup plans and alternate ways to solve any issues and ensure the seamless execution of the craft fair expansion.

Maintain open, transparent communication with stakeholders during the craft fair growth process. Keep suppliers, sponsors, attendees, and community partners updated on the expansion plans, timetables, and significant achievements. Seek feedback and input from stakeholders to resolve issues, solicit recommendations, and assure their involvement and support for the expansion. Develop solid connections with stakeholders to promote collaboration and alignment with the craft fair's goals.

Consider the possibility of sustainable and long-term growth by spreading the artisan fair to numerous venues. Consider market saturation, audience demand, competitiveness, and scalability when determining the possibility of long-term growth in each place. Create ways to track the performance and effect of the craft fair's expansion over time and adjust the approach as needed to maximize long-term growth and sustainability.

Ensure legal and regulatory compliance while extending the craft show to several sites. Understand the local laws, permits, licenses, zoning rules, and insurance needs for each site. Obtain the required permissions and licenses, such as event permits, food handling permits, alcohol permits, and insurance coverage, to guarantee that the craft fair operates in line with local standards and that guests and merchants are safe and secure.

Expanding the craft fair to numerous venues has a significant influence on the local community and demonstrates a commitment to social responsibility. Investigate possibilities to give back to the community through nonprofit partnerships, contributions, or community service projects related to the craft fair. Engage with local stakeholders, including residents, businesses, and community groups, to better understand their wants and concerns and incorporate their feedback into the growth strategy.

Extending a craft fair to other sites involves careful planning, financial management, risk reduction, stakeholder engagement, sustainability planning, legal compliance, and social responsibility. By taking a complete strategy and addressing critical concerns, organizers may effectively extend their craft fair to various sites while providing great experiences for guests, merchants, and the community as a whole.

Diversifying Event Offerings

Diversifying event offerings is a strategy approach that entails broadening the range of events, goods, and experiences available at a craft fair in order to attract a larger audience, improve the attendee experience, and generate more income.

Here's a thorough look at how organizers might vary event offerings:

1. Craft Categories: Increase the number of craft categories available at the craft fair to cater to a broader range of interests and preferences. Consider including classic crafts like pottery, woodworking, and textile arts, as well as more modern crafts like digital art, eco-friendly products, and repurposed items. Diversifying craft categories ensures that the craft fair appeals to a wide range of preferences and interests.

2. Artisan Demonstrations: Include artisan demonstrations and live crafting workshops to provide audiences with an immersive and instructive experience. Invite talented artists to exhibit their craft methods, give insights into their creative process, and interact with audiences via hands-on workshops and demonstrations. Artisan demos enhance the craft fair by allowing guests to learn new skills and develop a greater appreciation for handcrafted items.

3. Interactive Workshops: Provide interactive workshops and DIY-creating stations so participants may engage in hands-on crafts and produce their own handcrafted items. Collaborate with local artists, craft specialists, and DIY instructors to provide classes on a number of themes, including jewelry making, candle making, painting, and paper crafts. Interactive workshops provide visitors with a unique and memorable experience while encouraging creativity and skill development.

4. Food and Beverage Vendors: Include food and beverage vendors in the craft fair to improve the gastronomic experience for guests. Collaborate with local culinary artisans, food trucks, and specialized vendors to provide a wide menu of artisanal food and drinks. Consider offering gourmet snacks, unique beverages, and locally sourced items that match the craft fair concept and appeal to foodies.

5. Live Entertainment: Add to the mood of the artisan fair by showcasing live performances such as music, street performers, and interactive entertainment. Hire local artists, bands, and performers to offer live music and entertainment during the event. Create specific performance spaces or stages where people may relax, enjoy the entertainment, and soak in the joyful spirit of the artisan fair.

6. Youngsters' Activities: Make the craft fair more family-friendly by providing activities and entertainment for youngsters. Create specific children's spaces with age-appropriate crafts, games, and activities to keep young attendees involved and delighted. Consider collaborating with local organizations or companies to provide children's workshops, face painting, storytelling sessions, and interactive activities tailored to various age groups.

7. Artisanal Food Market: Establish an artisanal food market or culinary showcase that offers locally sourced, handmade food goods and gourmet treats. Invite artisanal food makers, specialized merchants, and gourmet artists to show off their products and provide samples to guests. Create a separate food court or tasting area where participants may taste and buy artisanal foods, gourmet snacks, and specialized delights.

8. Theme Events and Special Features: To increase attendance and interest, incorporate themed events, unique features, or curated experiences into the craft fair. Consider themes such as seasonal festivals, cultural festivities, or current events that resonate with the target audience and are consistent with the craft fair's goal and ideals. To improve the premium experience for select guests, consider adding additional elements like VIP activities, exclusive shopping hours, or VIP lounges.

Scaling Up Operations for a Craft Fair

Scaling up operations for a craft fair means carefully extending the event's size, breadth, and reach to accommodate expansion, attract more guests and merchants, and increase overall efficiency.

Here's a thorough look at how organizers might grow operations.

1. Venue Expansion: Expand the event venue or obtain more space to accommodate a larger number of exhibitors and guests. Assess possible locations based on capacity, accessibility, amenities, and cost. Consider indoor and outdoor venues, convention halls, parks, and other appropriate places that can handle the craft fair's desired size.

2. Logistical Planning: Create detailed logistics strategies to successfully manage operations on a larger scale. Coordinate transportation, parking, and traffic flow to accommodate more people and provide easy access to the venue. Plan for additional staffing to handle registration, security, vendor support, and other operational activities. Implement effective logistical systems to simplify setup, takedown, and event operations.

3. Vendor Recruitment: Increase the number of vendors participating in the craft fair by aggressively recruiting artisans, crafters, and makers from a greater geographic region and across many craft categories. Develop focused vendor recruiting techniques to attract high-quality exhibitors and ensure that the event showcases a varied range of products and crafts. Provide merchants with support and assistance to help them participate and have a better experience at the craft fair.

4. Marketing and Promotion: Expand your marketing and promotion activities to reach a bigger audience and raise awareness and interest in the craft show. Expand your marketing channels and methods to include digital marketing, social media advertising, email marketing, print advertising, local media partnerships, and community outreach programs. Create captivating marketing messaging and creative material to attract guests while highlighting the craft fair's unique characteristics and products.

5. Community Engagement: Work with the local community and stakeholders to generate support and excitement for the enlarged craft fair. Collaborate with area companies, organizations, and community groups to publicize the event and encourage participation. Seek out chances for cross-promotion, sponsorship, and collaboration with local influencers and community leaders to boost marketing efforts and reach a larger target audience.

6. Technological Integration: Integrate technological solutions to enable expanded operational scale while also improving guest and vendor experiences. Use event management software, smartphone applications, and online registration systems to simplify event planning, ticketing, and registration. Use technology for communication, marketing, and guest engagement to efficiently manage the broader event.

7. Financial Management: Expand financial management systems to properly handle additional revenues, costs, and financial transactions related to the larger craft show. Create strong financial planning, budgeting, and accounting procedures to assure openness, accountability, and compliance with financial rules. Implement financial systems and controls to track and manage cash flow, revenue sources, and event-related costs.

8. Operational Efficiency: Concentrate on improving operational efficiency to accommodate the expanded size of operations while providing a seamless and delightful experience for attendees and vendors. Implement optimized processes, workflows, and procedures for effective event logistics, vendor coordination, attendee registration, and customer service management. Invest in training and development programs to provide staff and volunteers with the skills and knowledge required to properly manage a major event.

Sustainability and Community Participation in Hosting a Craft Fair

Sustainability and community participation are critical components of hosting a craft fair, ensuring its long-term viability, beneficial environmental effect, and meaningful relationship with the local community.

To reduce environmental impact and promote responsible purchasing, craft fairs should incorporate sustainable practices into their planning and implementation.

Organizers can implement a variety of sustainable projects, such as: Eco-Friendly Techniques:

Implementing eco-friendly techniques like trash reduction, recycling, and the use of compostable or biodegradable items can help reduce the event's environmental effects. Encourage suppliers to adopt environmentally friendly packaging materials and decrease single-use plastics.

Energy Efficiency: Choose energy-efficient lighting and equipment, use renewable energy whenever available, and urge suppliers to implement energy-saving techniques. Take steps to limit energy use during the event, such as turning off lights and equipment while not in use.

Waste Reduction: Provide recycling and composting bins, encourage guests to bring reusable bags and containers, and reduce the usage of disposable products. Work with local waste management groups to guarantee appropriate trash disposal and recycling of items.

Sustainable Transportation: Encourage attendees and exhibitors to use sustainable modes of transportation, such as public transit, cycling, carpooling, or walking, to decrease carbon emissions connected with event travel. Provide incentives for eco-friendly transportation, such as preferential parking for carpoolers or discounts for guests who take public transit.

Community interaction is crucial for forging relationships, generating support, and providing a feeling of belonging at craft fairs.

Here are some ways to participate in the community:

Collaborate with Local Organizations: Work with local community organizations, nonprofit groups, schools, and cultural institutions to promote the craft fair, engage the community, and highlight local talent and efforts. Collaborative activities may include holding community workshops, art displays, or cultural performances as part of the event.

Volunteer chances: Provide chances for community members to assist in the preparation and implementation of the craft fair. Volunteering not only helps with event logistics, but it also instills a sense of ownership and community pride in participants.

Community Outreach: Use community outreach activities to generate knowledge about the craft fair and encourage participation from a varied range of community members. Use local media, community newsletters, social media platforms, and neighborhood groups to publicize the event and attract a larger audience.

Cultural Inclusion: Celebrate the community's cultural variety by adding parts of local culture, customs, and legacy to the craft fair program. Showcase craftsmen from diverse ethnic origins and encourage cultural interchange and appreciation.

Community advantages: Emphasize the craft fair's good influence on the local community by demonstrating economic advantages, supporting local craftsmen and companies, and contributing to community development projects. Communicate the event's dedication to sustainability, diversity, and social responsibility in order to establish its community worth.

Implementing Sustainable Practices in Craft Fair

Implementing sustainable practices is critical to ensuring that a craft fair has a low environmental impact, encourages responsible consumerism, and contributes to the well-being of the community and the world.

Here's an in-depth look at how craft show organizers may incorporate sustainable practices into their planning and execution:

1. Location Selection: Choose a location that values sustainability and adheres to environmentally friendly ideals. Seek out venues with green certifications, such as LEED, that show a dedication to energy efficiency, water conservation, and waste reduction. Consider sites that provide public transit or bike lanes to encourage guests and vendors to use sustainable modes of transportation.

2. Waste Reduction: Use waste reduction tactics to reduce the quantity of garbage produced during the craft show. Encourage merchants and guests to utilize reusable, recyclable, or compostable packaging, cutlery, and containers. Provide properly labeled recycling and composting containers throughout the venue to help with appropriate trash disposal and recycling.

3. Energy Efficiency: To maximize energy efficiency, use energy-efficient lighting, equipment, and appliances throughout the craft show. To decrease energy usage, use LED lighting, energy-efficient HVAC systems, and Energy Star-rated appliances. Turn off lights and equipment when not in use, and use natural light wherever feasible to save energy.

4. Water Conservation: Take water-saving measures to limit water consumption during the craft fair. Use water-saving fixtures and appliances in restrooms and food service areas to reduce water waste. Encourage vendors to adopt water-saving measures, such as employing water-efficient dishwashing methods and minimizing water consumption for cleaning and cooking.

5. Transportation: Encourage guests and sellers to use sustainable modes of transportation when getting to the craft fair. Encourage carpooling, public transit, cycling, and walking by giving information on alternate modes of transportation and incentives for environmentally responsible travel. Consider providing bike racks, dedicated carpool parking, or shuttle services to encourage sustainable mobility.

6. Food and Beverage: Look for locally made, organic, and sustainably sourced food and drinks for the craft fair's concessions and merchants. Choose merchants who stress sustainable practices, such as using seasonal goods, eliminating food waste, and providing vegan choices. Encourage suppliers to use compostable or biodegradable serving utensils to reduce single-use plastic.

7. Education and Outreach: Use education and outreach programs to raise knowledge of sustainability and environmentally friendly practices among attendees, vendors, and staff. Provide information on sustainable practices, such as waste reduction, energy and water conservation, and support for local artists and companies. Provide educational programs, demonstrations, and interactive activities that encourage sustainability and environmental care.

8. Collaboration and Partnerships: Work with local organizations, environmental groups, and sustainability projects to strengthen the craft fair's sustainability efforts. Partner with environmentally conscious vendors, sponsors, and suppliers who share the event's dedication to sustainability. Collaborate with community stakeholders to create sustainable practices and projects that benefit both the environment and the local community.

By incorporating sustainable practices into all aspects of the craft fair, organizers can create an environmentally responsible event that adheres to eco-friendly principles, educates attendees and vendors on sustainability, and demonstrates a dedication to protecting the planet for future generations.

Local Communities Engagement in Craft fair Sustainable Practice

Engaging with local communities is critical to the success and sustainability of a craft fair. Building strong ties with the surrounding community not only improves the event's reputation, but it also promotes a sense of belonging, support, and cooperation.

Here's a thorough look at how organizers may effectively interact with local communities:

To organize a successful craft fair, it's important to understand the local community's needs, beliefs, and interests. Engage with community residents, local businesses, neighborhood groups, and cultural organizations to learn about the community's preferences, demographics, and priorities. This insight will help shape event planning decisions and customize the craft fair to the needs and expectations of the local community.

Establish collaborations with local organizations, companies, schools, and community groups to expand the craft fair's reach and effect. Collaborate with local craftsmen, crafters, and manufacturers to promote their skills and goods throughout the event. Collaborate with local companies to sponsor the craft fair, offer in-kind assistance, or participate as vendors. Collaborate with schools and youth groups to engage young artists and promote creativity in the community.

Involve the community in organizing, promoting, and executing the craft fair to foster ownership and participation. Gather input and comments from community members via surveys, focus groups, and community meetings to ensure that their opinions are heard and respected during the event preparation process.

Recruit volunteers from the local community to help with the craft fair's different parts, including event preparation, hospitality, and logistics.

Proactively promote the craft fair in the community to increase awareness and participation. To promote the event and attract a larger audience, use a range of communication channels, such as local media, community newsletters, social media platforms, and neighborhood groups.

Attend local community events, festivals, and markets to promote the craft fair and interact with people of the community in person.

The craft fair aims to promote cultural inclusion and diversity by highlighting the local community's creative diversity and rich heritage. Encourage involvement from craftsmen of many ethnic origins, traditions, and artistic forms. Include cultural performances, demonstrations, and exhibitions that highlight the community's variety and foster cross-cultural understanding and respect.

Communicate the craft fair's beneficial influence on the local community to build support and excitement. Highlight the event's economic advantages, such as supporting local craftsmen and companies, creating income for the community, and drawing tourists to the region.

Emphasize the social and cultural advantages, such as increasing community pride, encouraging innovation, and creating community relationships via shared experiences.

By actively engaging with local communities, organizers may develop a craft fair that represents the community's distinct character and values, promotes cooperation and inclusion, and adds to the general well-being and vibrancy of the place.

Craft Fair Arrangement in Supporting Small Business and Craftsmen

Supporting artists and small companies is an important component of arranging a craft fair since it allows these individuals to expose their abilities, creativity, and handcrafted items to a larger audience.

Here's a thorough look at how craft fairs may effectively help craftsmen and small businesses:

1. Platform for Exposure: Craft fairs provide an excellent opportunity for craftsmen and small businesses to acquire exposure and attention for their products. Craft fairs allow craftsmen to present their handcrafted wares to a wide range of participants, including potential buyers, retailers, and fellow artisans. This exposure may help craftsmen develop their consumer base, raise brand awareness, and build relationships within the artisan community.

2. Sales and money generation: Craft fairs offer craftsmen direct sales possibilities to increase money and sustain their livelihoods. Craft fairs allow craftsmen to sell their handcrafted goods and put the revenues back into their enterprises. Craft fairs provide a retail setting in which craftsmen may meet with clients, tell the stories behind their items, and form relationships that can lead to repeat business and word-of-mouth recommendations.

3. Networking and Collaboration: Craft fairs provide opportunities for craftsmen, small companies, and industry experts to connect and collaborate. Participating in craft fairs helps craftsmen meet other makers, share expertise and resources, and form supportive ties within the artisan community. Craft fairs also allow artisans to cooperate with other vendors, merchants, and organizations to broaden their reach, enter new markets, and work on joint ventures or creative initiatives.

4. Market Research and Feedback: Craft fairs provide wonderful opportunities for craftsmen to perform market research and solicit feedback from consumers and guests. Craft fairs allow craftsmen to contact clients directly, providing them with real-time feedback on their items, price, and presentation. This input enables craftsmen to better understand client preferences, recognize market trends, and make educated decisions to enhance their goods and marketing tactics.

5. Professional Development: Craft fairs provide opportunities for artists to grow professionally and enhance their skills. Craft fairs provide craftsmen with valuable experience in marketing, sales, customer service, and event management. Craft fairs offer a hands-on learning environment in which craftsmen may hone their business abilities, learn from other vendors, and obtain insight into industry best practices.

6. Community Support and Recognition: Craft fairs help to raise awareness of and support for local craftsmen and small businesses. By hosting and attending craft fairs, community members show their support for local craftsmen and small businesses, which contributes to the local economy's vibrancy and variety. Craft fairs also provide an opportunity for craftsmen to receive recognition and appreciation for their skills, creativity, and contributions to the community's cultural fabric.

7. Promotion and Marketing: Craft fairs provide chances for artisans to promote and sell their products to a larger audience of prospective clients. Craft fair organizers frequently engage in marketing and advertising to attract participants and develop discussion about their events. This marketing exposure benefits craftsmen by improving product recognition and attracting visitors to their craft fair booths. Furthermore, artists may use social media, email marketing, and other digital platforms to promote their presence at craft fairs and draw buyers to their booths.

Craft fairs help artisans and small companies by providing opportunities for exposure, sales, networking, market research, professional growth, community support, and marketing. Organizing and participating in craft fairs allows craftsmen to demonstrate their skills, interact with clients, and contribute to the lively ecosystem of handcrafted items and small-scale enterprises.

Building Long-Term Partnerships With In the Craft Fair Communities

Building long-term partnerships is critical to a craft fair's continued success and expansion. These ties go beyond individual transactions, instilling loyalty, trust, and mutual support among organizers, suppliers, attendees, sponsors, and the broader community.

Here's a thorough look at how to create and nurture long-term connections in the setting of a craft fair:

Establishing trust and credibility among craft show stakeholders is crucial for building long-term partnerships. Organizers should conduct their contacts with vendors, attendees, sponsors, and community partners with professionalism, honesty, and integrity. Organizers may gain the trust and confidence of all parties involved by regularly following through on pledges, adhering to ethical standards, and keeping open communication lines.

Open communication is essential for establishing and maintaining long-term connections in the craft show industry. Organizers should promote open and honest communication with vendors, attendees, sponsors, and community stakeholders. This involves delivering regular updates, requesting input, immediately responding to complaints and grievances, and actively listening to all stakeholders' needs and recommendations. By allowing for two-way contact, organizers may improve connections and demonstrate their commitment to responsiveness and responsibility.

Organizers should prioritize providing concrete advantages to vendors, attendees, sponsors, and the community to build long-term connections. This includes allowing vendors to showcase their products, offering attendees unique experiences and attractions, providing sponsors with marketing exposure and brand visibility, and positively contributing to the local community through economic, social, and cultural initiatives. By continually providing value and advantages, organizers may foster loyalty and support from all stakeholders.

Craft fairs encourage community engagement among merchants, participants, sponsors, and supporters. Organizers should aggressively promote community participation by providing chances for stakeholders to meet, collaborate, and network. This involves planning community events, workshops, and activities that bring people together while instilling a feeling of belonging and togetherness. Organizers may foster a strong sense of community, resulting in a friendly and inclusive atmosphere that fosters ongoing engagement and involvement.

To preserve long-term connections, organizations must adapt and evolve to shifting stakeholder demands and preferences. This entails constantly analyzing market developments, soliciting input, and adjusting tactics and products accordingly. Organizers should be proactive in resolving difficulties, capitalizing on opportunities, and innovating to improve the craft fair experience for all stakeholders.

By exhibiting flexibility and agility, organizers may deepen connections while ensuring the craft fair's long-term relevance and success. Organizers may foster long-term connections within the craft fair community by focusing on trust, communication, value creation, community participation, and adaptation. These relationships provide the foundation for long-term success, growth, and good influence.

Giving Back To the Community

Giving back to the community is an important component of arranging a craft fair since it helps organizers positively touch the local region and have a lasting impact beyond the event.

Here's a thorough look at how craft fairs may give back to their communities:

Craft fairs may help support local issues and nonprofits by donating a part of event revenues or fundraising efforts to community projects, philanthropic initiatives, or groups in need. Organizers can engage with local NGOs to promote awareness about their concerns, provide them with a platform to display their work, and generate funding through donations or joint fundraising efforts during the craft fair.

Craft fairs promote economic growth by supporting local craftsmen, manufacturers, and small companies. Craft fairs boost economic activity in the community by giving a forum for these entrepreneurs to present and sell their products. They also produce cash for local craftsmen and vendors and contribute to the local economy.

Craft fairs can draw people from outside the region, resulting in increased spending at local shops, restaurants, and lodging. Craft fairs promote creativity and creative expression by allowing local craftsmen to display their handcrafted products and abilities. Craft fairs promote and celebrate the community's distinctive creative culture, inspiring creativity, supporting local artists, and encouraging artistic business. This has the potential to positively enhance the community's cultural vibrancy and identity.

Craft fairs promote community participation by allowing local individuals to participate as merchants, volunteers, or attendees. By actively incorporating the community in the craft fair's planning, advertising, and execution, organizers may instill a sense of ownership and pride in attendees. Craft fairs may also act as a meeting place for residents to meet, mingle, and enjoy their local arts and culture.

Craft fairs may serve the community by providing seminars, demonstrations, and educational events promoting artisanal skills, traditional crafts, and DIY culture.

These programs enable community members to gain new skills, express their creativity, and participate in hands-on learning experiences. Craft fairs can also work with local schools, libraries, and community centers to increase access to educational programs and resources.

Craft fairs may promote environmental stewardship through sustainable practices and eco-friendly activities. Organizers may decrease trash, lower the carbon impact, and promote recycling and composting at the event.

Craft fairs can also collaborate with local environmental organizations to enhance environmental awareness, promote sustainable living habits, and support community conservation initiatives.

Craft fairs contribute to the community by supporting local causes and nonprofits, promoting economic development, encouraging creativity and artistic expression, engaging with the community, providing educational outreach and programming, and demonstrating environmental stewardship. By embedding these activities into the fabric of the craft fair, organizers may have a long-term positive influence on the community's well-being and vibrancy.

Sample Vendor Application Form

To participate in a craft fair, merchants must usually fill out a vendor application form. This form allows organizers to obtain vital information on possible vendors and their products, ensuring that the event is consistent with the general theme and quality requirements. Here's an example of how a prototype vendor application form may look:

Vendor Application Form

Business   Name:

____

Contact   Information:

____

—

Phone   Number:

____

Email   Address:

____

Website   (if   applicable):

____

Social media handles (if applicable):

Business address:

City: _________________________________ State:
__________. Zip code is ______________.

Product/Service Types Offered:

Please give a brief description of your firm and the products/services
you provide:

____

____

____

____

Have you ever attended any craft fairs or similar events? If so, please
share details:

____

____

Please include information about the items or services you want to sell at the craft fair. Include information like cost, materials utilized, and any unique characteristics.

Please include images or examples of your products/services (if available).

[Please attach photographs or examples here.]

Please specify the size of your booth space:

[] Standard Booth Space (10'x10')

[] Double booth area (20'x10').

[]   Custom   size   (please   provide   dimensions):

____

Do you need access to electricity for your booth? [] Yes [] No

Do you have any specific needs or demands for your booth setup? If so, please specify:

____

____

____

____

Please mention your chosen payment method for booth fees:

[ ] Credit Card [ ] Check [ ] Cash

By signing below, you indicate that you have read and agree to comply by the rules and regulations of the craft fair:

Signature: ____ Date:
____

Please send this completed application form together with any applicable fees or papers to the organizers by the stipulated time.

Please note: Submission of this application does not guarantee admission as a vendor at the craft show. Organizers have the right to assess all submissions and make final selections based on considerations such as product quality, diversity of products, and overall fit with the event concept.

Thank you for your interest in participating in our craft show. We look forward to examining your application and maybe having you as a vendor at our event!

[End of Application Form]

This sample vendor application form includes critical facts regarding the vendor's business, products/services, booth needs, and payment choices. It helps organizers to examine the viability of the vendor for the craft fair and provide a varied and high-quality range of items for guests.

Craft Fair Venue Check List

A venue checklist is a must-have tool for craft fair organizers when organizing and carrying out their events. It ensures that all essential preparations are completed for a successful event at the designated location.

Here is a full summary of what a venue checklist may include:

To select a venue for a craft fair, first confirm availability for the chosen dates. Determine the venue's viability using criteria such as size, layout, accessibility, amenities, and parking availability.

Determine logistical requirements, such as load-in and load-out hours, vendor and attendee parking, and utility access. Work with venue management to handle any special logistical requirements or constraints.

Layout and Setup: Develop a design for vendor booths, lanes, registration/check-in areas, food and beverage stations, bathrooms, and other event elements. Ensure that the venue layout promotes efficient traffic flow and maximizes space use. Identify and secure event-related equipment and supplies, including tables, chairs, tents, signs, trash, and recycling containers.

Schedule the delivery, setup, and removal of equipment and supplies before and after the craft show.

To ensure safety and security, do a venue inspection to identify any potential dangers or problems. Make sure emergency exits are properly marked and easily accessible, and keep first aid supplies and emergency contact information on hand. Implement security measures as appropriate, such as hiring security guards or working with local law enforcement.

To operate a craft fair, get the necessary permits and licenses from municipal authorities, including event permits, health permits for food vendors, and alcohol permits (if applicable).Ensure enough insurance coverage is in place to cover responsibility and any hazards involved with organizing a craft show.

 Get event liability insurance and any other coverage necessary from the venue or local authorities.

Provide venue data, setup instructions, load-in/load-out hours, parking information, and other pertinent logistics to participating vendors. Give merchants clear instructions and expectations for booth layout, product display, and conduct at the craft fair.

Accessibility and Accommodations: Make the facility accessible for all guests, including those with impairments. Make arrangements for people who may need special assistance, such as wheelchair-accessible toilets or seating places

.Cleaning and Maintenance: Work with venue personnel or cleaning services to keep the facility clean and well-maintained before, during, and after the craft fair. Schedule frequent trash pickup and cleaning of communal areas throughout the event.

Marketing and Promotion: Promote the craft fair using social media, email newsletters, local advertising, and community outreach. Make sure the venue's address, directions, parking information, and event schedule are prominently displayed in marketing materials.

Provide services for vendors, including parking, beverages, bathrooms, and break places. Ensure that merchants have access to energy, if necessary, to power their booth setup.

Engage with the local community to promote the craft fair and increase attendance. Collaborate with area companies, organizations, and community groups to improve the event experience and increase community participation.

A venue checklist helps organizers plan and manage the logistical, operational, and promotional aspects of organizing a craft fair in a specific location. By carefully addressing each item on the checklist, organizers can guarantee that the event runs smoothly and successfully, meeting the demands of vendors, visitors, and the local community.

Craft Fair Marketing Material Templates

Marketing material templates are critical tools for advertising a craft fair and recruiting merchants and guests. These templates serve as guidance for creating various promotional materials, ensuring that branding and messaging are consistent across all media.

 Here's a full breakdown of typical marketing materials templates used for craft fairs:

1. Flyer Template: Use a flyer template to design eye-catching promotional flyers for distribution in high-traffic areas, such as local businesses and community centers. The template normally contains room for event information such as the date, time, and location, as well as a brief description of what people may anticipate at the craft fair. It may also include photographs or sketches of handcrafted items to draw attention.

2. Poster Template: A poster template is similar to a flyer template but built for bigger print sizes. Organizers can use it to create posters that will be prominently displayed on street poles, bulletin boards, or business windows. The template contains room for event details and images that draw the viewer's attention from a distance.

3. Social Media Graphic Template: These templates help create promotional visuals for Facebook, Instagram, and Twitter. The template usually includes room for event information, interesting

imagery connected to the craft fair, and branding components like logos and color schemes. Organizers have tailored these visuals for social media sharing to generate buzz and enthusiasm about the event.

4. Email Newsletter Template: Use an email newsletter template to create promotional emails for potential attendees and vendors. The design has areas for event information, vendor highlights, special deals or discounts, and a call-to-action to RSVP or register for the event. It may also include photographs or testimonials from previous craft shows to help establish credibility.

5. Press Release Template: Use this template to create an official notice for the craft fair and send it to local media, newspapers, and internet publications. The template includes sections for event information, history of the craft show and its organizers, quotations from important players, and media contact information. Press releases are an efficient way to get media attention and raise awareness for an event.

6. Vendor Application Form Template: Although not a marketing tool, a vendor application form template is crucial for inviting merchants to participate in the craft fair. The template offers areas where vendors can enter information about their company, products or services, booth needs, and payment options. It also provides

directions for submitting the application and any necessary papers or costs.

Using these marketing materials templates, craft fair organizers may design professional, unified promotional pieces that successfully explain the event's value and promote participation from both exhibitors and guests. These templates make the design process easier and guarantee that marketing activities are uniform and effective across all platforms.

Financial Spreadsheets for Craft Fair

Financial spreadsheets are crucial tools for craft fair organizers to use while planning, tracking, and managing the financial elements of their event. These spreadsheets assist event organizers in estimating expenditures, projecting income, and maintaining financial records throughout the planning and implementation process.

Here's a full description of the several sorts of financial spreadsheets usually used when beginning a craft fair:

1. Budget spreadsheet: This spreadsheet outlines the projected expenditures for arranging the craft show. It is divided into categories such as venue rental fees, equipment rental or purchase, marketing and promotion charges, permits and licenses, insurance, staff or volunteer expenses, and miscellaneous costs. Organizers may enter expected expenditures for each category and track actual spending to ensure that the event stays on budget.

2. Revenue projection spreadsheet: Organizers can use this spreadsheet to estimate prospective profits from the craft fair. It includes vendor booth fees, ticket sales (if applicable), sponsorships, concessions, and any other revenue streams. Organizers can enter predicted income figures for each category based on previous statistics, market research, or expected attendance.

3. Expense Tracking spreadsheet: This spreadsheet records and monitors real expenditures spent during the craft fair planning and implementation process. It has columns for noting the date of spending, description, category (e.g., venue, marketing, supplies), amount spent, and payment method. Organizers may use this spreadsheet to monitor costs in real time and compare them to the budget to find overspending or inconsistencies.

4. Vendor Fee Calculation Worksheet: The vendor fee computation worksheet determines the costs charged to participating merchants for booth space at the craft fair. It considers booth size, location (e.g., indoor vs. outdoor), amenities (e.g., access to electricity), and any other services provided (e.g., promotional possibilities). Organizers may enter these parameters into the spreadsheet to find the best cost structure for vendors based on their individual requirements and preferences.

5. Financial Summary Spreadsheet: This spreadsheet summarizes the craft fair's financial performance, including total sales, costs, net income/loss, and other important measures. It combines data from the budget, revenue prediction, and spending tracking worksheets to create a complete picture of the event's financial situation.

6. Profit and Loss Statement (P&L): A profit and loss statement outlines the craft fair's financial performance over a certain time period, which is usually the duration of the event. It accounts for income earned, costs expended, and the net profit or loss made by the craft fair. Organizers can use this statement to evaluate the event's profitability and highlight areas for future improvements.

Craft fair organizers may use these financial spreadsheets to efficiently plan, manage, and analyze the event's finances, ensuring financial sustainability and success. These spreadsheets offer significant insights into the event's financial health, assisting organizers in making educated decisions and facilitating open communication with stakeholders such as suppliers, sponsors, and financial partners.

Conclusion

Running a craft fair involves rigorous preparation, excellent organization, and a thorough grasp of all elements of event administration, marketing, and financial management. Throughout this book, we've looked at the key procedures and considerations for launching and running a successful craft fair.

We started by talking about the craft fair business environment, including its development, trends, and prospective prospects for ambitious organizers. Understanding market demand, competition, and target audience is critical for creating a distinctive and exciting event that appeals to both vendors and attendees. We then went into the practical components of event preparation, such as research and planning, venue selection, logistics, vendor acquisition and management, marketing and promotion, financial management, and community involvement. Each of these aspects is critical to the craft fair's success and long-term survival.

Throughout the planning phase, organizers must stress good communication, attention to detail, and the ability to react to changing conditions. Building solid connections with vendors, sponsors, local communities, and guests is critical for instilling a sense of belonging and maintaining the event's long-term success.

Financial management is an important component of hosting a craft fair; organizers must carefully budget, analyze costs, and forecast earnings to ensure financial viability. Financial spreadsheets and tools can assist organizers in properly planning, monitoring, and evaluating the event's financial performance.

Ultimately, the success of a craft fair is dependent on the organizers' ability to provide a unique and memorable experience for both merchants and consumers. By emphasizing quality, innovation, and community participation, craft fair organizers may create a successful event that honors local craftsmen, stimulates creativity, and enhances the community.

As organizers consider the design and execution of a craft fair, they should get input from participants and stakeholders, assess the event's performance, and identify areas for improvement. This continual process of reflection and improvement is essential for the craft fair's long-term evolution and growth.

Creating a craft fair is a gratifying undertaking that involves hard work, ingenuity, and a strong desire to assist local craftsmen and small businesses. By adhering to the concepts and techniques mentioned in this book, ambitious organizers may lay the groundwork for a successful and meaningful craft fair that will become a treasured neighborhood institution for years.

www.ingramcontent.com/pod-product-compliance
Lightning Source LLC
Chambersburg PA
CBHW051602250726
48653CB00004BA/1293